MIDDLE EAST NATIONS IN THE NEWS

Saudi Arabia
IN THE NEWS
PAST, PRESENT, AND FUTURE

David Schaffer

MyReportLinks.com Books
an imprint of

Enslow Publishers, Inc.
Box 398, 40 Industrial Road
Berkeley Heights, NJ 07922
USA

To Nancy, Helena, and Lily Jane

MyReportLinks.com Books, an imprint of Enslow Publishers, Inc. MyReportLinks® is a registered trademark of Enslow Publishers, Inc.

Library of Congress Cataloging-in-Publication Data

Schaffer, David.
  Saudi Arabia in the news : past, present, and future / David Schaffer.
     p. cm. — (Middle East nations in the news)
  Includes bibliographical references and index.
  ISBN 1-59845-026-3
  1. Saudi Arabia—Juvenile literature. I. Title. II. Series.
  DS204.25.S33 2005
  953.8—dc22

                              2005022205

Printed in the United States of America

10 9 8 7 6 5 4 3 2 1

To Our Readers:
Through the purchase of this book, you and your library gain access to the Report Links that specifically back up this book.
The Publisher will provide access to the Report Links that back up this book and will keep these Report Links up to date on **www.myreportlinks.com** for five years from the book's first publication date.
We have done our best to make sure all Internet addresses in this book were active and appropriate when we went to press. However, the author and the Publisher have no control over, and assume no liability for, the material available on those Internet sites or on other Web sites they may link to.
The usage of the MyReportLinks.com Books Web site is subject to the terms and conditions stated on the Usage Policy Statement on **www.myreportlinks.com.**
A password may be required to access the Report Links that back up this book. The password is found on the bottom of page 4 of this book.
Any comments or suggestions can be sent by e-mail to comments@myreportlinks.com or to the address on the back cover.

Photo Credits: Al-Islam.org, p. 31; All Rights Reserved for Ministry of Education © 2004, p. 44; AP/Wide World Photos, p. 1; Central Intelligence Agency, pp. 6 (flag), 97; © BBC, pp. 17, 38; © BBCM-MVI, pp. 34, 106; © Corel Corporation, pp. 10, 19, 29, 35, 53, 72, 83, 100, 110; © Devillier Donegan Enterprises, p. 94; © KRSH&RC 2003, p. 67; © 1983–2005 Martin Gray, All Rights Reserved, p. 46; © 1995–2005 WGBH Educational Foundation, p. 12; © 1996–2005 National Geographic Society, pp. 69, 74; © 2000–05 Pearson Education, p. 15; © 2002 ArabNet, p. 65; © 2002 Heights Productions, Inc., p. 55; © 2003, Jaringan Islam Liberal, p. 48; © 2003 Saudi Gazette, p. 20; © 2005 Information Office of the Royal Embassy of Saudi Arabia in Washington, p. 90; © 2005–03 The National Museum, p. 76; © 2005 The American-Israeli Cooperative Enterprise, p. 99; © 2005 Time, Inc., p. 108; © 2006 Cable News Network LP, LLLP, p. 26; © 2006 MacNeil/Lehrer Productions, p. 59; Enslow Publishers, Inc., p. 5; Explore Saudi Arabia, p. 86; Katrina Thomas/*Saudi Aramco World*/PADIA, pp. 3 (soccer players), 40, 63; Library of Congress, pp. 7, 42, 57, 80, 92, 105; M.S. Al-Shabeeb/*Saudi Aramco World*/PADIA, pp. 3 (man dancing), 50; MyReportLinks.com Books, p. 4; Peter Harrigan/*Saudi Aramco World*/PADIA, p. 61; Photos.com, p. 33; Smithsonian National Museum of Natural History, p. 78; S. M. Amin/*Saudi Aramco World*/PADIA, p. 116; The Saudi Arabia Information Resource, p. 102; The White House, p. 6 (Abdullah and Cheney); Tor Eigeland/*Saudi Aramco World*/PADIA, p. 28; United Nations Global Teaching and Learning Project, p. 114; University of Texas Libraries, pp. 13, 24; U.S. Department of State, p. 112.

Cover Photo: AP/Wide World Photos

Cover Description: Muslim pilgrims on hajj at the Kaaba in Mecca, Saudi Arabia.

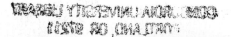

Contents

Boys playing soccer

Jiddah dance

MyReportLinks.com Books
Great Books, Great Links, Great for Research!

The Internet sites featured in this book can save you hours of research time. These Internet sites—we call them **"Report Links"**—are constantly changing, but we keep them up to date on our Web site.

When you see this "Approved Web Site" logo, you will know that we are directing you to a great Internet site that will help you with your research.

Give it a try! Type **http://www.myreportlinks.com** into your browser, click on the series title and enter the password, then click on the book title, and scroll down to the Report Links listed for this book.

The Report Links will bring you to great source documents, photographs, and illustrations. MyReportLinks.com Books save you time, feature Report Links that are kept up to date, and make report writing easier than ever! A complete listing of the Report Links can be found on pages 118–119 at the back of the book.

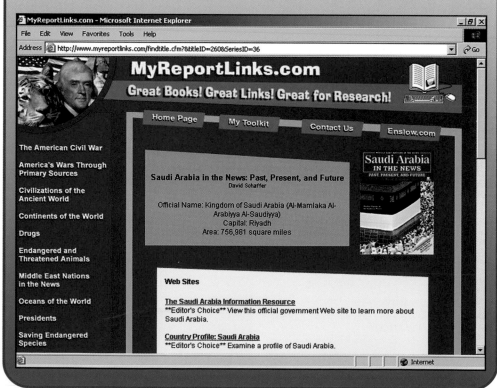

Please see "To Our Readers" on the copyright page for important information about this book, the MyReportLinks.com Web site, and the Report Links that back up this book.

Please enter **NSA1429** if asked for a password.

▲ Map of Saudi Arabia

Saudi Arabia Facts

Flag
Green, a traditional color in Islamic flags, with the Shahada or Muslim creed in large white Arabic script (translated as "There is no god but God; Muhammad is the Messenger of God") above a white horizontal saber (the tip points to the hoist side).[1]

Official Name
Kingdom of Saudi Arabia (Al-Mamlaka Al-Arabiyya Al-Saudiyya)

Capital
Riyadh

Population
26,417,599
(July 2005 est.)

Area
756,981 square miles

Highest Point
Jabal Sawda, 10,279 feet

Lowest Point
Persian Gulf, 0 feet

Location
Middle East, bordering the Persian Gulf and the Red Sea, north of Yemen and south of Iraq

Type of Government
Monarchy

Head of State
King and Prime Minister Abdullah bin Abd al-Aziz Al Saud

Head of Government
King and Prime Minister Abdullah bin Abd al-Aziz Al Saud

Monetary Unit
Saudi riyal (SAR)

Official Language
Arabic

National Anthem
Aash Al Maleek ("Long Live Our Beloved King")

King Abdullah II and Vice President Cheney

Time Line

A.D. 570—The Prophet Muhammad is born in Mecca.

c. 1500—The Saud family takes control of a small territory near present-day Riyadh.

1700s—Wahhabi Islam spreads throughout the Arabian peninsula. The Saud family helped and supported this movement.

1891—The Ottoman Empire and various tribes gain control of much of the Arabian peninsula.

1902—Saud family, led by Abd al-Aziz ibn Saud, conquers the Najd, Hasa, Asir, and Hejaz regions of Arabia to form the Kingdom of Saudi Arabia.

1932—*September 23:* Kingdom of Saudi Arabia is officially unified.

1933—Petroleum production begins in Saudi Arabia.

1967—Israeli forces led by Ariel Sharon invade Lebanon in an attempt to push the Palestine Liberation Organization (PLO) away from the border.

1973—Saudi Arabia cuts shipments of oil to Western nations to protest Western support of Israel in another Arab-Israeli War.

1975—King Faisal of Saudi Arabia is assassinated. His half brother, Prince Khalid, takes the throne.

1982—Khalid is succeeded by his half brother, Prince Fahd.

1991—Saudi Arabia and a coalition of nations led by the United States defeat Iraq in the Persian Gulf War.

2005—*August 1:* Abdullah bin Abd al-Aziz Al Saud becomes King of Saudi Arabia.

Khalid and Faisal

Chapter 1 ▶

Modernism, Islamic Tradition, and Terrorism

As news broke following the terrorist attacks of September 11, 2001, it was learned that fifteen of the nineteen hijackers had come from Saudi Arabia. Osama bin Laden, suspected of masterminding the attacks, is also of Saudi origin. The Saudi government, though, stripped him of his citizenship in 1994.

Saudi Arabia had long been viewed as a moderate Arab state friendly to Western nations. Now, the country came to be seen in a more critical and suspicious way by many Americans and others throughout the world. Journalist and Arabic studies specialist James Wynbrandt explains the reaction to the 9/11 suicide hijackings as it concerns Saudi Arabia:

> The tragic events of September 11, 2001, planned and perpetrated in the main by Saudi-born terrorists, have raised questions about what role the kingdom plays in the spread of international terrorism, and whether Saudi Arabia is a friend or foe of the West, and in particular the United States.[1]

▲ *This is an aerial view of Dhahran, Saudi Arabia. Dhahran is a city made up of employees that work for Aramco. Many of those living there are foreign workers with jobs in the oil industry.*

Doubts were later raised about the identities of the hijackers. It seemed some of them may have used stolen identities. This meant they might not be Saudi natives after all. It was also clear that people involved with terrorism came from many other countries, not just Saudi Arabia. There was no sign that the Saudi government had played any role in the attacks. Still, negative perceptions of Saudi Arabia quickly spread.

Sources of Saudi Extremism

Then again, there is widespread support in Saudi Arabia for violence against foreigners. This is particularly true of non-Muslims occupying Arab lands, such as the Hebrews in Israel. Saudi people regard terrorism as a fair way to fight against the presence of foreign, non-Muslim forces on sacred Muslim and historic Arab territory. The United States and other Western nations have kept a strong presence in the Middle East for many years. That presence is largely seen as anti-Arab and anti-Muslim by the local people.

Strong sentiment against outside influences is common throughout the Middle East, but especially so in Saudi Arabia. The two most holy sites of Islam, the cities of Mecca and Medina, are both in Saudi Arabia. Both cities are off-limits to non-Muslims. Furthermore, the form of Islam practiced in Saudi Arabia is one of the most fervent and strict. Known as Wahhabi Islam, it is observed by an overwhelming majority of Saudis. Wahhabism, called Tawhid by the Saudis, was introduced by the Al Saud ruling family. It is the only form of religion legally allowed to be practiced in Saudi Arabia.

The laws of Wahhabi Islam call for following Islamic beliefs and practices as they existed in the days of the Prophet Muhammad, the founder of Islam. He lived from roughly A.D. 570 to 632. Interpreting or changing Islamic beliefs based on modern developments is wholly rejected. There is no allowance for the practice of other religions or refraining from religious practices.

Intense pressure to follow the rules of Wahhabism has long been common within Saudi Arabia. But some Saudis believe that they are also justified in taking action against non-Muslim

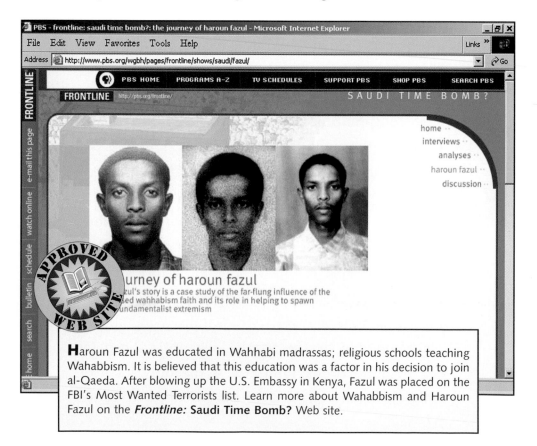

Haroun Fazul was educated in Wahhabi madrassas; religious schools teaching Wahabbism. It is believed that this education was a factor in his decision to join al-Qaeda. After blowing up the U.S. Embassy in Kenya, Fazul was placed on the FBI's Most Wanted Terrorists list. Learn more about Wahabbism and Haroun Fazul on the *Frontline: Saudi Time Bomb?* Web site.

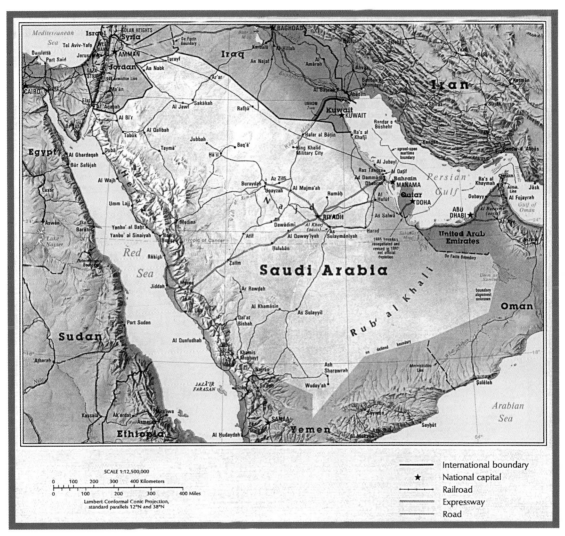

▲ A map of Saudi Arabia from 1993.

foreigners as well. These feelings have grown as Saudi Arabia has become increasingly engaged in trade partnerships and military alliances with non-Arab and non-Muslim nations. The clash in principles and values between the modern, non-Muslim Western world and that of Wahhabi Islam is perhaps illustrated no better than by some members of the royal Al Saud family itself.

Mixing Modernism and Conservative Islam

The Al Saud family has ruled parts of Saudi Arabia for over two centuries. It has ruled what is now known as Saudi Arabia since the beginning of the twentieth century. The Al Saud family has been most responsible for asserting Wahhabi control over Saudi Arabia. The Al Saud family were early followers of Wahhabi Islam. In the eighteenth century they formed an alliance with a religious scholar named Muhammad ibn Abd al-Wahhab, the founder of Wahhabi Islam. The Al Saud clan agreed to use their military strength to help establish a unified Arab nation based on the very conservative form of Islam Ibn Abd al-Wahhab preached.

It took nearly two hundred years for the Al Saud family to finally gain total and permanent control over Saudi Arabia, but they would never waver from their firm commitment to Wahhabi Islam. When Saudi control was finally established,

Wahhabi Islam was imposed as the only officially sanctioned religion in the country.

However, as Saudi Arabia has grown prosperous and moved into the modern, globally connected world, the Al Saud family has had problems living up to Wahhabi standards. Many Wahhabi religious leaders have regarded the use of any technology or knowledge not available at the time Muhammad lived as forbidden. Trying to meet that standard would have made it impossible for Saudi Arabia to develop its energy industry, its transportation and communications networks, and its sleek, modern city centers. Ruling members of the Al Saud family have often defended becoming a more modern

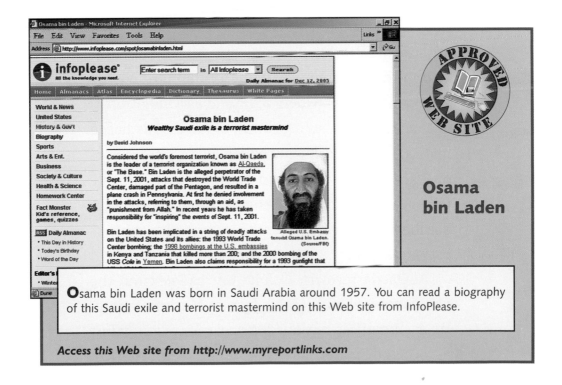

Osama bin Laden was born in Saudi Arabia around 1957. You can read a biography of this Saudi exile and terrorist mastermind on this Web site from InfoPlease.

Access this Web site from http://www.myreportlinks.com

nation with new technology by claiming this benefits the promotion of Islam.

Religious leaders and devotees in Saudi Arabia have not always agreed with the Al Saud family. Yet, for many decades they were willing to accept the Al Saud clan as their national leaders. However, these feelings seemed to shift following the placement of large numbers of Western troops in Saudi Arabia during the Gulf War against Iraq in 1990.

▶ Foreign Forces on Sacred Soil

When the Saudi government agreed to let foreign troops be stationed in Saudi Arabia to fight against Iraq, many Saudi people who had accepted or supported the Al Saud rulers came to question their authority. Allowing foreign, non-Muslim fighters into the nation that was home to the most sacred sites of Islam was widely regarded as a violation of Islamic Law. The ruling family's power was based upon their being devout believers and promoters of Wahhabi standards and values. Therefore, the public view of them as straying from those standards and values presented them with serious problems.

Al-Qaeda terrorist Osama bin Laden cited the occupation of Saudi Arabia by non-Muslim foreigners as one of his reasons for declaring war against the United States and the West in the 1990s.

Wahhabi Islam is the officially sanctioned religion of Saudi Arabia. This article from the BBC provides a brief look at this form of Islam.

Access this Web site from http://www.myreportlinks.com

However, resentment and hostility over foreign occupation were not sentiments felt only by violent extremists in the Arab world. How this troop deployment provoked negative reaction among the Saudi people is described by Wynbrandt: "The request for U.S. protection incensed many Saudis. . . . While many other Saudis saw the necessity of the military arrangement, however distasteful, young religious scholars denounced having 'infidels' protect the home of Islam."[2]

▶ The Beginning of the Terror War

Anti-Western sentiment intensified as United States troops remained in Saudi Arabia long after the war ended. For the first time, terrorist groups with Saudi and Wahhabi origins attacked government targets within Saudi Arabia and Western targets around the world. Since the end of the first Gulf War, terrorists have launched attacks in the United States, Spain, Pakistan, and Indonesia. The Indonesian attack took place at a resort visited by many Australians. Spain, Pakistan, and Australia all supported the United States in its war against terrorists in Afghanistan and Iraq. Saudi Arabia has also been attacked several times, and several Americans as well as Saudis have been killed or wounded in those attacks. The worst of these occurred in May 2003, when suicide bombers in Riyadh killed thirty-five people. Hundreds of people were injured in earlier attacks in 1995 and 1996.

▶ Ties to Terrorism

It is troubling for the Saudi government to come under terrorist attacks at home while being blamed internationally for supporting terrorism. This criticism became stronger as it became known that many Saudi nationals, including powerful private citizens and members of the government, had been providing aid to terrorist organizations for a long time. At first, the United States also supported some of these organizations. In the 1980s, the United States government backed radical Muslims that were fighting against the Soviet Union. As time went on, these groups shifted to become terrorist organizations. Robert Baer, a former CIA official involved with antiterrorist operations, describes allegations that came out about connections between prominent Saudis and terrorists following the 9/11 attacks:

▲ *The oil industry is a source of both great wealth and great turmoil in Saudi Arabia. Some Saudis resent the high salaries earned by foreign workers that come to work in Saudi Arabia.*

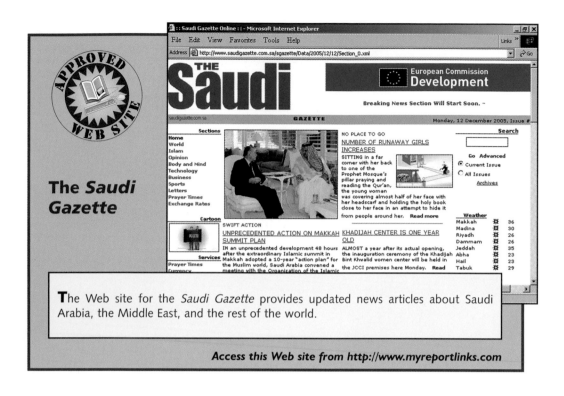

:: Saudi Gazette Online :: - Microsoft Internet Explorer

File Edit View Favorites Tools Help   Links »

Address http://www.saudigazette.com.sa/sgazette/Data/2005/12/12/Section_0.xml   Go

THE Saudi
GAZETTE

European Commission
Development

Breaking News Section Will Start Soon. ~

Monday, 12 December 2005, Issue #

The Saudi Gazette

Sections
Home
World
Islam
Opinion
Body and Mind
Technology
Business
Sports
Letters
Prayer Times
Exchange Rates

Cartoon

Services
Prayer Times
Currency

NO PLACE TO GO
NUMBER OF RUNAWAY GIRLS INCREASES
SITTING in a far corner with her back to one of the Prophet Mosque's pillar praying and reading the Qur'an, the young woman was covering almost half of her face with her headscarf and holding the holy book close to her face in an attempt to hide it from people around her. **Read more**

SWIFT ACTION
UNPRECEDENTED ACTION ON MAKKAH SUMMIT PLAN
IN an unprecedented development 48 hours after the extraordinary Islamic summit in Makkah adopted a 10-year "action plan" for the Muslim world, Saudi Arabia convened a meeting with the Organization of the Islamic

KHADIJAH CENTER IS ONE YEAR OLD
ALMOST a year after its actual opening, the inauguration ceremony of the Khadijah Bint Khwalid women center will be held in the JCCI premises here Monday. **Read**

Search
Go Advanced
Current Issue
All Issues
Archives

Weather
Makkah   36
Madina   30
Riyadh   26
Dammam   26
Jeddah   35
Abha   23
Hail   23
Tabuk   29

The Web site for the *Saudi Gazette* provides updated news articles about Saudi Arabia, the Middle East, and the rest of the world.

Access this Web site from http://www.myreportlinks.com

The wife of the Saudi ambassador to the United States had handed out money that found its way to two of the 9/11 hijackers. A raid on the Hamburg [Germany] apartment of a suspected accomplice of the hijackers had turned up the business card of a Saudi diplomat. The two hijackers who arrived in Los Angeles were met by a Saudi working for a company contracted to the [Saudi] ministry of defense. Other Saudis fed the ATM machines for the hijackers.[3]

With accusations like these emerging, international favor for the Saudi regime dropped, just as internal discontent with them was rising.

Internal Discontent and Tension

Saudi Arabia's rulers have other problems at home. There are imbalances within Saudi society between different economic and social classes. This has caused resentment of the ruling class and contributed to tensions within Saudi Arabia. There is also resentment among many Saudi people toward foreigners from the United States and European countries who have been brought into the country to work. Some of these foreign workers have been brought in to handle highly skilled jobs for which, for many years, Saudis were not adequately educated. Others have been brought in to handle menial or domestic service jobs considered undesirable by many Saudi people. Both of these groups have made some in the native population feel encroached upon, even violated, as many of the foreigners are not Muslim and do not observe the strict customs and practices of the local Saudi people.

The role and rights of women is also a difficult issue for the leaders of Saudi Arabia. Saudi Arabia is one of the most conservative nations in the world in terms of what rights it allows women. Women usually receive less education than men and have less career opportunity. Women's activities and movements within Saudi Arabia are very limited. For example, they are not permitted to drive and cannot travel without a male relative's consent. They must dress in very conservative clothing that covers nearly their entire bodies, including their hair and faces. Social contact between men and women who are not related is forbidden. This discourages many businessmen from interacting with women, and doing business with them.

Like other oppressed groups in Saudi Arabia, women have recently begun to speak out. The government has responded positively in some cases, but changes to existing Saudi policies are usually opposed by hard-core Wahhabi leaders, who enjoy popular support. Efforts by the government to bring about social change and progress therefore often serve to heighten tensions within Saudi Arabia rather than reduce them.

Given all the pressures it faces both at home and internationally, some question if the Saudi monarchy can continue to keep power in Saudi Arabia. Given how dependent much of the world is on Saudi energy resources, the country's great strategic importance, and its historical role as the sacred land of Islam, questions about the fate of Saudi Arabia and what kind of government is in control there weigh heavily on the entire world.

Chapter 2

Land, Climate, and Ecology

For many people, the words Saudi Arabia conjure up images of vast, barren desert. The nation's climate and environment almost entirely match these images. Most of Saudi Arabia's land is sandy and dry. Temperatures are generally very high. The average summer temperature is about 113°F. East and west coastal areas have slightly lower temperatures but also very high humidity. Daily winter temperatures average about 60–75°F, but night temperatures in the interior deserts sometimes drop below freezing. Strong northerly winds can also help give the desert air a sharp chill in winter.

Rainfall averages only about four inches per year in the whole of Saudi Arabia, but some areas go years with no rainfall at all. The climate along the west coast is more temperate and moist, receiving about ten to twenty inches per year. Severe sandstorms driven by powerful winds often cover large portions of the country. Saudi Arabia is so dry that there are no permanent lakes, rivers,

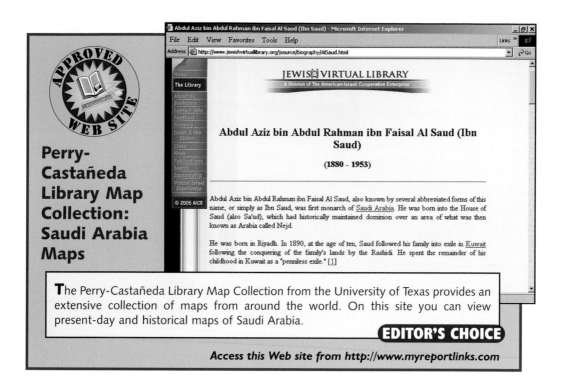

Perry-Castañeda Library Map Collection: Saudi Arabia Maps

The Perry-Castañeda Library Map Collection from the University of Texas provides an extensive collection of maps from around the world. On this site you can view present-day and historical maps of Saudi Arabia.

EDITOR'S CHOICE

Access this Web site from http://www.myreportlinks.com

or other bodies of freshwater anywhere in the country. At times runoff water flows through what are usually dry riverbeds remaining from prehistoric times, creating temporary freshwater bodies called wadis. There are also freshwater springs scattered around Saudi Arabia. Water from the wadis, springs, and water pumped from underground have actually enabled Saudi Arabia to produce considerable agricultural activity in certain regions.

Size and Boundaries

Covering 756,981 square miles, Saudi Arabia is about one fifth the size of the United States. It is bordered by the Red Sea to the west; the nations of Jordan, Iraq, and Kuwait to the north; the Persian Gulf and the nations of Qatar and United Arab Emirates to the east; and the nations of Oman and Yemen to the south. The emptiness of much of Saudi Arabia's extreme desert spaces has led to great uncertainty concerning the nation's exact borders. Since the early twentieth century, Saudi Arabia has had numerous border disputes with some of its neighbors, including Kuwait, Yemen, and Iraq. The borders between Saudi Arabia, Oman, and the United Arab Emirates in the Al Buraymi oasis area are still unresolved. This is one of the few places in the world where borders between nations are uncertain.

The Hejaz and Najd Regions

There is regional diversity within Saudi Arabia. The areas of the country that are farthest to the west experience a lesser degree of heat and dryness. This is due to moisture from the Red Sea and higher elevations. The Hejaz region in the northwest is more temperate in climate, receives considerably more rainfall, and is more fertile than most of the country. It is here that large-scale settlement first took place in Saudi Arabia. The large, ancient cities of Mecca and Medina are located in the Hejaz. They are critically important to Saudi Arabia both commercially

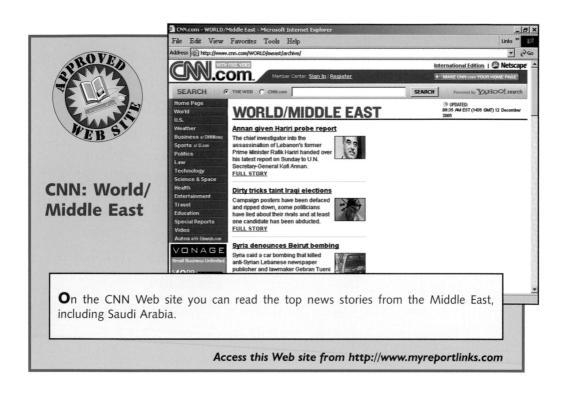

CNN: World/ Middle East

On the CNN Web site you can read the top news stories from the Middle East, including Saudi Arabia.

Access this Web site from http://www.myreportlinks.com

and culturally. So is the major port city of Jeddah.

In the central region of the country lies the Najd Plateau. This area is a mixture of deserts and scattered mountain ranges. Much of the land surface within Najd is rocky and dry, but a ring of mountains called the Jabal Tuwayq in southern Najd includes many oases. Large modern cities have grown around here, including the capital city of Riyadh. Other large cities in the Najd are Buraydah, Hail, and Unayzah.

The Hejaz and Najd have historically been the largest and most significant regions of Saudi Arabia. There has also been a history of tension and conflict between them. Wynbrant elaborates in *A Brief History of Saudi Arabia:*

> The relations between Hejaz, the more settled and traveled region along the west coast, and Najd, the arid interior dominated by Bedouins [nomadic tribespeople], were frequently hostile. Hejaz exhibited the influence of a succession of outside rulers . . . as well as that of untold numbers of pilgrims. Najd had never come under foreign domination or influence, and its people regarded themselves as the more authentic Arabian culture.[1]

Mountains, Deserts, and Coastal Lands

The Asir region in the southwest is characterized by mountains that are considerably cooler than the rest of the country. Some peaks in this area reach a height close to ten thousand feet above sea level. Rainfall averages about twenty inches per year, far higher than the national average. Average daily temperatures are only about 67°F. A narrow coastal plain between the mountains and the Red Sea is one of Saudi Arabia's most agriculturally productive areas. Similarly, the area just to the east of the mountains also has substantial agricultural activity. Two major wadis, the Bishah and the Tathlith, are major sources of water for this area. Major cities include the Red Sea port of Jizan, and Najran, an important crossing point along the border with Yemen.

▲ *These Saudis are visiting an oasis in the desert dear Dhahran.*

At the eastern end of the Najd plateau lies the Ad Dahna desert. This is a narrow strip of desert that runs from north to south, and is sometimes called the River of Sand. Only a few isolated oasis areas exist between the Ad Dahna and the coastal plain along the Persian Gulf. Al Hasa, with its main settlement of Al Hufuf, is the largest and most fertile oasis area in the eastern Arabia area known as Eastern Province. The region is in fact generally referred to as Al Hasa. Along the Gulf coast, massive sand flats and shallow waters shift frequently. In the northern part of this region, the land is more gravel laden and somewhat more stable. The world's busiest oil shipping port, Ras Tanura, is in the Eastern Province. Other major cities include Dhahran and Dammam, which are also important to the oil industry.

The Al Hasa region is the largest oasis on the eastern portion of the Arabian Peninsula. This is an image of the village of Marat in the Al Hasa region of the Najd.

There are two vast desert regions in Saudi Arabia. The largest and most desolate of these is the Rub al Khali in the southeast. So barren and intense is this desert that much of it had never been explored or charted until the 1950s. Even then it was only with the help of satellite photographs from outer space. The Rub al Khali covers 212,356 square miles. The land surface in the west and central parts of the desert consists of fine and loose sands. These sands can rise up into huge clouds when blown by severe winds. The Rub al Khali is considerably smaller than the Sahara Desert of Africa, but it has much denser sand concentrations. The Rub al Khali is only about one seventh the size of the Sahara but has about half as much sand. Sand mountains of nearly a thousand feet sometimes form here.

▶ The Empty Quarter

To the east the land is more stable, with salt flats mixing with more stable sand, but throughout the region almost all of the land is uninhabitable. In fact, this portion of Saudi Arabia is so barren and untouched by humans that it is known as the Empty Quarter. The author of a 2005 *National Geographic* article describes how desolate the Empty Quarter is: "Because of these sandy expanses, not to mention its profound heat, the sands have long been judged too unforgiving for all but the most resourceful humans, considered more a wasteland to cross than a landscape to settle in."[2]

In northern Saudi Arabia lies the An Nafud, or Great Nafud. This desert lies in the area along the border with Jordan and Iraq. An Nafud is only about one tenth the size of the Rub al Khali. Some light vegetation sprouts here in the winter and early spring due to seasonal rains. Nomadic people live and graze their herds in parts of the An Nafud at this time of year. Nevertheless, An Nafud is mainly desert. Sand dunes in this desert reach to heights of several hundred feet. They stretch out in peaks and valleys for dozens of miles south of Saudi Arabia's northern border.

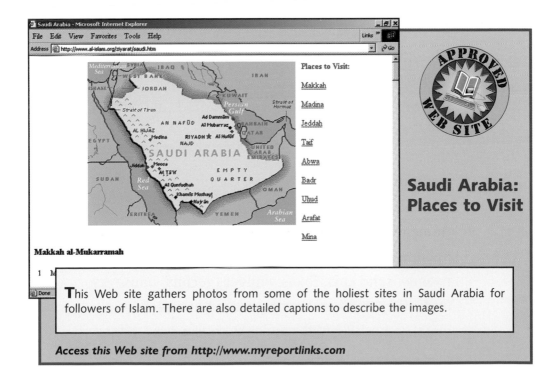

This Web site gathers photos from some of the holiest sites in Saudi Arabia for followers of Islam. There are also detailed captions to describe the images.

Access this Web site from http://www.myreportlinks.com

Plant Life

Desert plants like cactus and aloe can be found in much of Saudi Arabia. Flowers and trees grow almost exclusively in oasis areas or in the temperate climates along the coasts. The higher parts of the Asir contain some pine trees, and grasses and shrubs grow even in very dry areas during the brief rainy seasons. Date trees are abundant throughout Saudi Arabia's fertile areas. So common are date trees that one has been included on Saudi Arabia's coat of arms. Two plant products that Saudi Arabia has also been known for are frankincense and myrrh. They gained fame as gifts given to Jesus Christ upon his birth by the Eastern kings who traveled to the Middle East to witness it. Both substances are derived from the sap of trees that grow wild on the Arabian Peninsula. Myrrh was usually used in perfumes and cosmetics, while frankincense was burned as part of religious ceremonies.

Animal Life

Animal life is quite varied within Saudi Arabia. Baboons live in the southwestern Asir district. Bats abound in the central plateau region. Hedgehogs, hyenas, sand cats, foxes, wolves, gerbils, hamsters, and other mammals are present in much of the country. Endangered species such as oryx—a large desert-roaming antelope; ibex—a species of

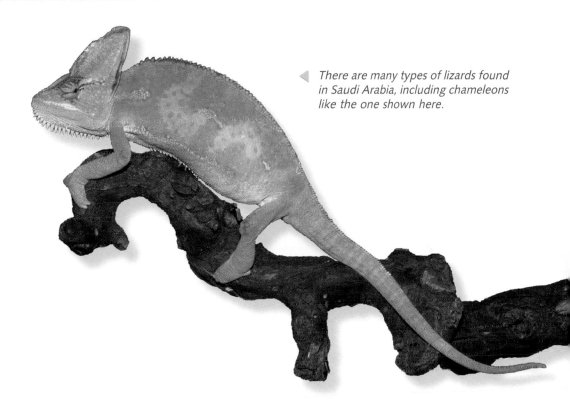

There are many types of lizards found in Saudi Arabia, including chameleons like the one shown here.

mountain goat, gazelles, and even ostriches have recently been reintroduced to the wild in Saudi Arabia. Camels once roamed wild in the desert but have been thoroughly domesticated. There are also dozens of varieties of snakes and lizards. One variety of lizard called the dhubb is especially suited to desert life and flourishes in Saudi Arabia. With no permanent bodies of freshwater, there are no fish or amphibian species living within Saudi Arabia. There are many kinds of local and migratory birds found in the country. Crows, sparrows, and black kites dwell permanently within Saudi Arabia. Waterfowl such as pelicans and flamingos live in the coastal areas. Migratory birds such as

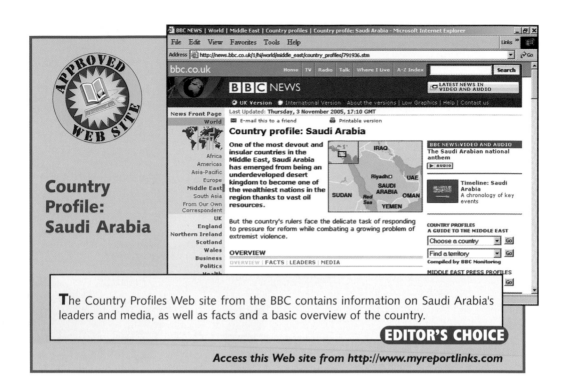

Country Profile: Saudi Arabia

The Country Profiles Web site from the BBC contains information on Saudi Arabia's leaders and media, as well as facts and a basic overview of the country.

EDITOR'S CHOICE

Access this Web site from http://www.myreportlinks.com

falcons and vultures, as well as doves, ducks, geese, owls, quail, and warblers pass through Saudi Arabia on their travel routes.

▶ Geology and Natural Resources

Wildlife may be limited to certain areas in Saudi Arabia now, but in ancient times it was wide-spread and diverse throughout the Arabian Peninsula. This land was under the ocean millions of years ago, and also has been moister and more temperate in climate in the past. Much of the wildlife that existed then left fossil deposits that have become crude oil. The presence of these oil supplies, the largest known oil deposits in the world, has had an enormous impact on Saudi Arabia.

Oil is not the only underground resource that has been important to Saudi Arabia. The nation also hopes to make use of vast natural gas supplies that also exist beneath its surface. The country has also had to resort to underground sources for much of its water. There are large amounts of water deep below Saudi Arabia's surface. Recent discoveries indicate there may be enough water to allow for much more irrigation and development

▲ *The oil industry in Saudi Arabia provides the people with many benefits, but occasionally some disasters. Petroleum tanks and refineries need to be located close to water, and sometimes mistakes occur that lead to oil spills that damage the water and sea life.*

on Saudi land. Saudi Arabia has also utilized seawater as a resource for irrigation and even drinking water. Desalination plants that remove salt from ocean water are located on Saudi Arabia's Persian Gulf coast. This dependence upon seawater led Iraqi leader Saddam Hussein to attempt to contaminate the supply by pumping crude oil into the Persian Gulf during the war against Iraq in 1991. He did this because the Saudis were aiding the coalition led by the United States. The Saudis managed to divert the oil away from the desalination plant.

Pollution

The waters of the Persian Gulf have also been badly polluted by crude oil spills and damage to oil tankers and facilities during the several military conflicts that have occurred there in recent years. Both the Saudi government and the energy companies that do business in that area have made efforts to clean up the gulf. Severe damage has been done to ocean life and the Gulf coast shorelines that has not been reversed by these cleanup efforts. There are oil-soaked birds, fish, and wildlife, as well as contaminated beaches. The extreme fire and air pollution hazards presented by massive amounts of exposed crude oil are among the most serious environmental concerns facing Saudi Arabia.

Chapter 3

Religion

The official religion of Saudi Arabia, and the only one that is allowed to be practiced openly, is Wahhabi Islam. As the government of Saudi Arabia bases its laws and policies on Wahhabi beliefs, the customs and practices of Islam are not only practiced by virtually every Saudi citizen, but they are enforced as law.

In the past there have been a variety of religions practiced on the Arabian Peninsula. Up until the seventh century A.D., there were Christians, Jews, and Zoroastrians living in what is now Saudi Arabia. Zoroastrianism was the religion of the ancient Persian Empire. All these religions were monotheistic, meaning belief in a single God. There were also pagan religions practiced in Saudi Arabia that believed in multiple gods. With the rise of Muhammad and Islam these pagan religions became forbidden. Other religions that recognized just one God were permitted in Arab territory for centuries after Muslims came to rule there. However, by the end of the eighteenth century, when the Al Saud clan started to gain control over large parts of what is now Saudi Arabia, that changed.

Not only were all religions other than Islam banned from being publicly practiced, so were all forms of Islam other than Wahhabi. There are a significant number of Shi'a Muslims, those that practice a variant of Islam more common in Iran and Iraq, in eastern Saudi Arabia. There is also a significant Shi'a community in the southern province of Najran. But they may not practice their religion openly. Shi'ites of Saudi Arabia have also historically suffered exclusion from the Al Saud-controlled government and discrimination

Religion & Ethics: Islam

Islam has been around for over thirteen hundred years. This Web site from the BBC contains an extensive amount of information on this religion.

Access this Web site from http://www.myreportlinks.com

in the job market. Some Saudi leaders have recently tried to improve conditions for the Shi'a minority, but overall they remain largely second-class citizens. Followers of Wahhabi Islam fully control the government and nearly every aspect of life in Saudi Arabia.

Muhammad and the Origins of Islam

The Islamic religion was started by the Prophet Muhammad in the A.D. 600s. Muhammad is recognized as one of the most influential people who have ever lived. In fact, historical author Michael Hart ranked Muhammad number one in his book *The 100: A Ranking of the Most Influential People in History*. "On the purely religious level . . . it seems likely that Muhammad has been as influential in human history as Jesus," says Hart. "Furthermore, Muhammad (unlike Jesus) was a secular as well as a religious leader."[1] Indeed, nowhere is Muhammad's impact on both government and religion more apparent than in Saudi Arabia, the land where he was born and lived his entire life.

Muhammad was born about A.D. 570 in the city of Mecca, which had been a major urban and trading center for many centuries. He was a member of the Quraysh tribe, one of the leading tribes in the area. Muhammad enjoyed noble status locally and his family lived comfortably, but he was beset by repeated tragedies at an early age. Both his

This boy is completing his morning prayer. Muslims must pray five times each day facing the holy city of Mecca.

parents died by the time he was six years old, and then his grandfather, who became his guardian, died within two years after that. Muhammad was then taken care of by his uncle, Abu Talib, who was a trade merchant. Muhammad traveled frequently with his uncle, becoming increasingly exposed to the various religions in the area that worshipped only one god. He became increasingly well known in Mecca as a trustworthy, honorable, and peaceful individual.

Later, Muhammad worked for a wealthy widow named Khadijah. She was very impressed with him. In spite of his being fifteen years younger, she proposed to him and they married. Khadijah would become the first convert to the new religion that Muhammad would form.

▶ Muhammad Becomes Religious

At that time, paganism as practiced by the central Arabian Bedouin was the most common religion throughout Saudi Arabia. A sacred black stone, kept in a holy shrine in Mecca known as the Kaaba—now the most sacred site of Islam—was at that time an important religious landmark and place where many people came on pilgrimages. But those who came were pagans. As Muhammad grew knowledgeable about various religions in the region, he became opposed to paganism and preferred the monotheistic approach of believing

▲ The Kaaba is a sacred shrine in Mecca that was a place for holy pilgrimages even before the founding of Islam. This photo of the Kaaba was taken around 1910.

in only one god. Muhammad believed that worshiping multiple gods led to moral and social decline, something that he felt had been occurring in Arabia during his lifetime.

The Revelations

Often Muhammad would seek out solitude to pray and meditate. One place he particularly liked was a cave on Mount Hira, just outside Mecca. It was here that Muhammad would have what he *were it was* claimed were revelations from God, or Allah, told *said that he was* to him by the archangel Gabriel. The revelations were regarding God's will and the proper method of worship for human beings. These revelations would become the basis for the beliefs of the Islamic religion.

Muhammad gained followers for Islam within Mecca, including several from his own family and tribe. However, there were those who disbelieved that Muhammad was receiving messages from God and considered him to be crazy. The strongest opposition came from leaders of the most power-ful clan within the Quraysh tribe. They feared that Muhammad's promotion of his new religion and his criticism of pagan beliefs would threaten the trade and commerce Mecca enjoyed from people visiting to see the Kaaba.

Because Muhammad belonged to the Quraysh tribe, his relatives, led by Abu Talib, were able to protect him. However, many of the people who followed his preachings were targeted by the city's leadership for punishment. As Muhammad became more outspoken against paganism and gained larger numbers of followers, other tribal leaders pressured Muhammad's family to stop protecting him. Facing severe opposition in Mecca, Muhammad sought a safer place for himself and his followers. He left Mecca in 622 after tribal leaders in the nearby city of Yathrib (later to be called Medina) pledged their support to Muhammad and agreed to follow his teachings.

Muhammad's journey to Medina came to be known as the Hegira. It was of critical importance in the development of Islam. It was in Medina

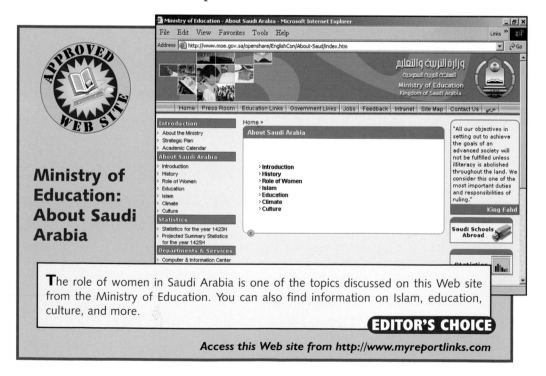

Ministry of Education: About Saudi Arabia

The role of women in Saudi Arabia is one of the topics discussed on this Web site from the Ministry of Education. You can also find information on Islam, education, culture, and more.

EDITOR'S CHOICE

Access this Web site from http://www.myreportlinks.com

that Muhammad and his followers would begin spreading Islam and build one of the largest empires in world history. The event of the Hegira was considered so important that it became the starting point of the Islamic calendar.

Islamic Supremacy

Once settled in Medina, Muhammad established himself as the most powerful person in the city: He had the support of both local leaders and those who had followed him from Mecca. He then spread his teaching to other areas of Arabia and looked to increase his realm of power. Often he achieved his goals through persuasion, preaching, and diplomacy. He also began advocating warfare as a just means of spreading Islamic power and the word of Allah as he interpreted it.

In A.D. 630, Muhammad sought to conquer the city of his birth, Mecca, and claim it in the name of Islam. Facing an army of ten thousand of Muhammad's followers, the leaders of Mecca ceded the city to Muhammad. He triumphantly returned to Mecca and converted it to Islam, smashing the pagan idols at the Kaaba. Muhammad treated the residents of Mecca humanely, which gained him even more followers. Furthermore, many more Arab tribal leaders also pledged their support to Muhammad once word spread that he was in control of the sacred city.

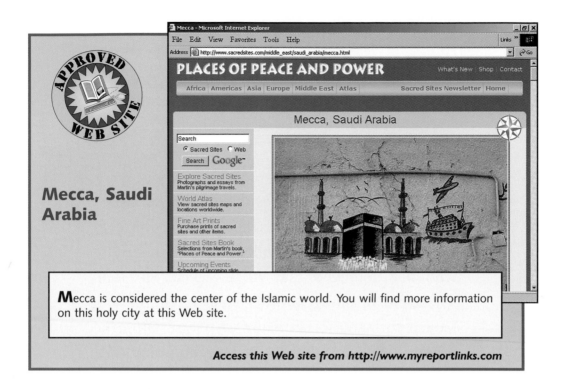

Mecca, Saudi Arabia

PLACES OF PEACE AND POWER

What's New | Shop | Contact

Africa | Americas | Asia | Europe | Middle East | Atlas   Sacred Sites Newsletter | Home

Mecca, Saudi Arabia

Search
Sacred Sites   Web
Search | Google

Explore Sacred Sites
Photographs and essays from
Martin's pilgrimage travels.

World Atlas
View sacred sites maps and
locations worldwide.

Fine Art Prints
Purchase prints of sacred
sites and other items.

Sacred Sites Book
Selections from Martin's book,
"Places of Peace and Power."

Upcoming Events
Schedule of upcoming slide

Mecca is considered the center of the Islamic world. You will find more information on this holy city at this Web site.

Access this Web site from http://www.myreportlinks.com

Muhammad continued military campaigns and added to Islam's sphere of influence. Even after his death in 632, Islam continued to spread, but it had already gained nearly unanimous support among Arabs by that time.

A Code for Worship and Governance

The words and teachings of Muhammad believed to have been revelations from God were compiled into a book called the Qur'an. This book is the basis of belief for the Muslim faith. Other sayings and actions of Muhammad, known as the Sunnah (tradition) of the Prophet, were passed on orally in the form of tales. The Arabic word for tales is

Hadith. About 250 years after Muhammad's death the Hadith that were considered genuine were collected and written down in "Hadith collections." Next to the Qur'an, they are considered to be the most important source of Islamic learning. These works lay down not just religious rules and teachings but also set standards of behavior for society and government.

The Rise of Wahhabism

The Wahhabi form of Islam was founded by a religious scholar from the Najd region named Muhammad ibn Abd al-Wahhab in the early eighteenth century. Some forms of Islam allow for Islamic law to be adapted to fit the needs of modern times. Wahhab Islam, however, calls for following the teachings of the Qur'an and Hadith collections absolutely. They cannot be modified or adapted.

This strict traditional interpretation of Islamic law that Ibn al-Wahhab supported came as a reaction against what he saw as pagan and un-Islamic practices on the part of many people in Arabia at that time. These included belief in the sacredness of inanimate objects such as plants and rocks, the calling on of saints and angels to help in personal pursuits, and offering animal sacrifices to god figures. Even the decoration of mosques and the adornment of tomb headstones were seen by

Wahhab as anti-Islamic. All of these practices were widespread in central Arabia during the years of Wahhab's upbringing and emergence as a religious leader. In fact, many Arabs, especially nomads and primitive tribal people, had never fully abandoned ancient spiritual beliefs and traditions. While Muslim in name, their actual religious behavior often more resembled that of the early followers of pagan religions.

Wahhabism started to gain a strong following in the Najd region in the mid-eighteenth century. Economic and social conditions declined in the area, causing discontent among tribal and regional leaders, who were tolerant of deviant religious

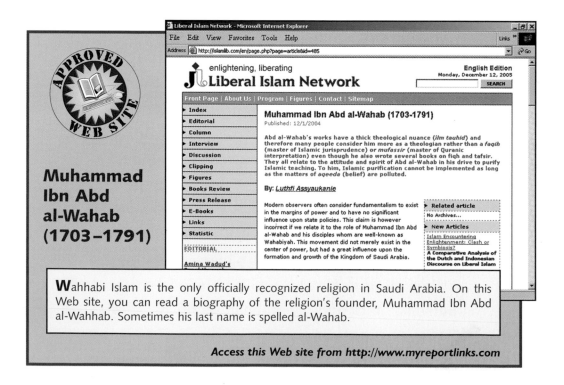

Muhammad Ibn Abd al-Wahab (1703–1791)

Wahhabi Islam is the only officially recognized religion in Saudi Arabia. On this Web site, you can read a biography of the religion's founder, Muhammad Ibn Abd al-Wahhab. Sometimes his last name is spelled al-Wahab.

Access this Web site from http://www.myreportlinks.com

and spiritual practices. Wahhab used this public discontent and claims of spiritual and moral superiority to gain a power base in Central Arabia. Some tribal and regional leaders came to support Wahhab. Among those leaders was the emir of Diriya, Muhammad ibn Saud, who in 1745 formed the alliance with Wahhab that would ultimately result in the modern nation of Saudi Arabia. By 1926, the Al Saud had succeeded in conquering the holy cities of Mecca and Medina in the Hijaz. They formally united the Hijaz with the Najd region into the Kingdom of Saudi Arabia in 1932. At this time, Wahhabi Islam was imposed on the entire population.

Islamic customs and practices in Saudi Arabia are the same or very similar to those practiced elsewhere in the world. However, because of the strictly conservative principles of Wahhabi Islam, these customs and practices are regarded with the utmost importance in Saudi Arabia and enforced rigorously.

▶ Religious Rites

For Muslims, prayer is a highly formalized and frequent occurrence. Five times a day Muslims must face in the direction of Mecca from wherever they are in the world and offer prayers to Allah, the Arabic word for God. Prayers are required at sunrise, midday, mid-afternoon, sunset, and before

▲ *This man is performing a Jiddah dance at the National Heritage and Folk Culture Festival. He is part of Saudi Arabia's National Guard. This festival was held to show how it was "in the days of our fathers and grandfathers." Followers of Wahhabi Islam seek to keep daily life as close as possible to how it was in the days of the Prophet Muhammad.*

retiring for the night. Daytime prayers are often recited in groups in public places, and attendance of prayer services at mosques is encouraged, especially for men. All Muslims are expected to attend the Friday noon prayer in a mosque, the Muslim day of rest. At all prayer meetings, men and women are kept separate, as they are in much of Muslim society.

Another important aspect of Islamic practice is the giving of charitable contributions (called Zakat). This is considered mandatory by Islamic teaching. In Saudi Arabia, the Zakat is levied as an official tax through the Saudi Arabian Zakat and Income Tax Authority. Money from practitioners goes to mosques and to aid the disadvantaged. Abstinence and fasting during the sacred month of Ramadan, the ninth month of the Muslim calendar, is also a vital part of the practice of Islam. During Ramadan, Muslims may not eat, drink, or smoke during daylight hours. Exceptions are made for the sick and feeble, pregnant women, and travelers. Whenever possible, these people are expected to make up for it at a later time.

▶ The Hajj

Making a pilgrimage to the Muslim holy city of Mecca during one's lifetime is another basic requirement of Islam. This pilgrimage, called the hajj, is made annually by millions of Muslims from around the world during the twelfth calendar month of the Islamic year. Since Mecca lies within Saudi Arabia, this journey is relatively easy for many Saudis.[2] Also, with both the holy cities of Mecca and Medina being in Saudi Arabia, the people of the country feel a special pride and dignity in being the keepers and protectors of these sacred sites.[3]

Diet, Dress, and Demeanor

Devotion to the Muslim faith is also reflected in what one eats and drinks, as well as clothing and appearance. Muslims are forbidden from eating pork; processed meats, such as sausage, that include animal blood; and certain kinds of exotic birds and seafood. Drinking alcohol is also not allowed for Muslims, and therefore, these products are illegal and unavailable in Saudi Arabia, except in sections of the country specifically designed and built to host foreigners living in the country. In these areas, drinking in the home is permitted. Clothing is also very conservative, and there are strong taboos against showing flesh in public. Men commonly wear large garments called thobes on their upper bodies that hang loose and long. Men also cover their heads with scarf-like cloths called gutras. As is common throughout the Muslim world, many men wear beards. Almost all women, Saudi and foreign,

These Saudis are sitting down for a traditional family meal.

appear in public fully covered from head to toe. The customary black garment Saudi women wear is called an *abaya*. Women also cover their heads and faces with cloths and veils.

Adherence to all the requirements of Islam is enforced not only by regular police but also by a special religious security force known as the *Mutawwa*. It is known for fiercely enforcing the

Wahhabi Muslim code of conduct and behavior. Those who violate it can expect to be interrogated, arrested, or even flogged by the mutawwain, who often work in conjunction with regular armed police. Clearly, whatever religious diversity or tolerance that once existed in Saudi Arabia is part of the past.

Chapter 4 ▶

Culture and Lifestyle

Like all aspects of life in Saudi Arabia, the nation's art, culture, and entertainment are mostly determined by the strict form of Islam followed there. Modern music, dance, and movies are all prohibited from public display or demonstration

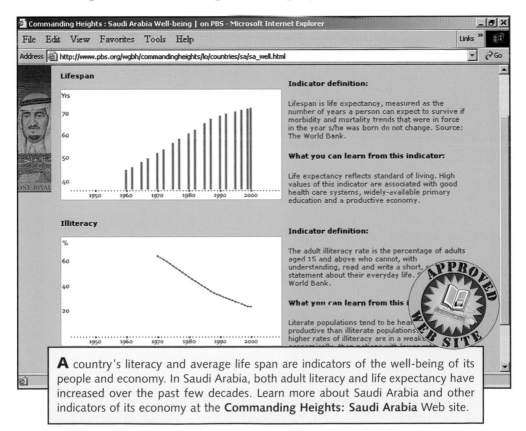

A country's literacy and average life span are indicators of the well-being of its people and economy. In Saudi Arabia, both adult literacy and life expectancy have increased over the past few decades. Learn more about Saudi Arabia and other indicators of its economy at the **Commanding Heights: Saudi Arabia** Web site.

in Saudi Arabia. Although there is television and radio in Saudi Arabia, they are also controlled by the government. Modern forms of art and culture that are popular and appreciated throughout the world are unavailable in Saudi Arabia.

On the other hand, in the past, the Arabian Peninsula has been a major producer of great works of literature, art, music, and dance. The great cultural traditions of Arabia were mostly established during a time when Islam held power over an expansive empire that was among the world's most cultured societies. The modern Saudi government and others in Saudi Arabia have shown a great interest in preserving the works from that period.

▶ Literature and Folklore

The Arabs have a rich literary tradition that predates the arrival of Islam. The classic poetry form known as the *Qasida,* or ode, adopted by Shakespeare and many other leading Western writers, was originated by Arab poets in the first millennium A.D. In pre-Islamic Arabia, poetry was an important form of oral communication as well as creative expression. News was passed using the ode. Oral histories and traditions were maintained within tribes and clans by recital of structured verse. Poetry was so important that competitions were conducted between members of different

▲ This image was created in 1873, during the days of the Ottoman Empire. It shows the traditional dress of some people living on the Arabian Peninsula.

clans and tribes. Great honor and esteem was bestowed upon the winners.

Many of the odes written in this period were romantic and tender, telling tales of love and valor. Among the most accomplished ancient Arab poets are Umar, Jamil, and Qays, also called Majnun Layla. These poets continue to be appreciated for their expressions of deep and passionate love, as well as for their eloquent use of the Arabic language. Other important pre-Islamic poets are Imru al-Qays and Amr ibn Kulthum.

More modern Saudi writing and literature is focused on Islamic religious teaching and the history of modern Saudi Arabia. An important writer of a more recent time is the Nadji historian Uthman ibn Bishr, who died in 1871 or 1872. He wrote about the early history of Saudi Arabia and the histories of the Al Saud clan and other leading Arab tribes. A well-known current Saudi author is Turki-al Hamad, who is famous for his trilogy of books featuring the main character Hisham al-Abir.

▶ Music and Dance

While the Saudi people have gained access to Western art and media through television, radio, and the Internet, they have usually shown a preference for traditional Arab forms. Many of the most popular modern songs in Saudi Arabia are based on the writings of famous ancient Arab poets. Arab folk music, usually consisting of a singer backed by string and percussion instruments, also remains very popular in Saudi Arabia. The enduring popularity of Arabian folk music is impressive, considering it originated many hundreds of years ago, in pre-Islamic days.

Other ancient forms of art and entertainment also remain popular in Saudi Arabia. Tribal and ancient religious dances are still admired and performed. In fact, these historic dances are the only kind of music or dance permitted to be performed in public. Only men can participate in these performances. The national dance of

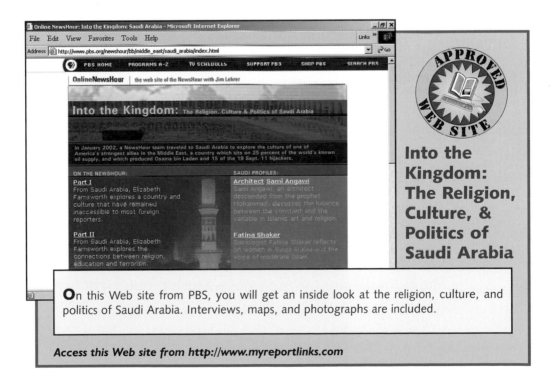

Into the Kingdom: The Religion, Culture, & Politics of Saudi Arabia

On this Web site from PBS, you will get an inside look at the religion, culture, and politics of Saudi Arabia. Interviews, maps, and photographs are included.

Access this Web site from http://www.myreportlinks.com

Arabia is called the *ardha*. Performing ensembles dress in colorful clothes and wave swords as they dance together in a line. Singers and drummers provide the musical backdrop for the dancers, and one singer narrates a story taken from an Arabic poem.

Visual Arts

One of the forms of art Arabs are most noted for is the method of decorative handwriting called calligraphy. Calligraphy originated in Saudi Arabia at the same time as the rise of Islam. Passages from the Qur'an and other Islamic writings have usually been the focus of Arabic calligraphy. Entire museum exhibits in Saudi Arabia are dedicated to calligraphy. Many Saudis study this art form, and there are numerous calligraphy competitions that draw great interest. Calligraphic inscriptions can be found on many public and religious buildings and decorative craft pieces.

Islamic architecture is also of high quality and admired throughout the world. Like calligraphy, architecture in Saudi Arabia was initially inspired by Islam. The most ornate and unique buildings in Saudi Arabia are the mosques—Muslim houses of worship. Mosques are usually domed on top, are fronted by pillars, and include tall slender towers known as minarets.

▶ Electronic Media

Modern forms of media and entertainment such as television, radio, and the Internet can be found in Saudi Arabia and have become popular. However, there has been resistance to the introduction of these technologies by strongly traditional Muslims. When Saudi Arabia's government television station first went on the air in 1965, there was widespread opposition and even riots. Saudi King Faisal received support from the country's

▲ Saudi Arabia did not have Internet access until 1999. By 2004, there were 2 million Internet users in the country. Al-Sakhra, or "The Rock," is one of many Internet cafes in the capital city of Riyadh.

top religious leaders to bring television to Saudi Arabia by pointing out it could be used to promote Islamic teaching. Saudi television remains geared heavily toward religious programming and is tightly controlled by the government. Still, Saudi citizens are able to view television stations from other countries, such as Qatar and the United Arab Emirates, whose governments are not as strict as Saudi Arabia's. Public radio stations have been broadcasting in Saudi Arabia since 1948, and like other Saudi media, the content on radio stations is almost wholly religious in subject matter. Public service broadcasts; programs on history, science, and politics; and even some music can also be found on Saudi radio stations. The music is either military or traditional Arabian folk. As with television, Saudis can also listen to radio stations from other, less restrictive countries.

The Internet

Internet traffic throughout Saudi Arabia has grown tremendously in a short time. The first Internet connection for the country, limited for use by research and academic organizations and some private companies, was made available in 1999. Five years later, there were dozens of Internet service provider companies in Saudi Arabia and nearly 2 million Internet users. The government monitors and censors all Internet transmissions that come across the country's phone and cable lines. Some Saudis manage to get around the restrictions by using satellite connections or international phone connections.

Yet for all the country's advances in technology, Saudis have shown that they prefer traditional Arabian tastes, styles, and customs. While accepting and even embracing modernization, the Saudi

▲ *Soccer is an incredibly popular sport in Saudi Arabia, just as it is in much of the world. These young boys are playing at the Al-Nahjah School in Hufuf.*

people have also shown they want to maintain their devout Islamic religious beliefs.

Sports and Entertainment

Like in many places of the world, soccer is a very popular sport in Saudi Arabia. The country has a national soccer team that participates in international competitions such as the Olympics and the World Cup. The team is well supported by the Saudi people, and there are soccer leagues and competitions for youth throughout the country. Saudi Arabian racehorses are considered among the best in the world, and horse racing is very popular in the country, as is camel racing. The King's Camel Race, held in the desert outside of Riyadh every year, is one of the nation's most popular events.

Also popular is a form of game hunting called falconry. In falconry, falcons are used to track and catch other birds and small animals. It is an ancient form of recreation still widely enjoyed in Saudi Arabia. Hunters carry falcons perched on their arm. The falcon's head is hooded until prey is spotted, then the hood is removed and the bird released to track and kill the targeted animal.

A sport that is relatively new to Saudi Arabia but growing quite quickly in popularity is golf. There was a large growth in the number of golf courses in Saudi Arabia during the 1990s. In spite of its harsh desert climate, Saudi Arabia has gone from just one golf course, first opened in the 1940s, to twenty today. Tennis and car racing are other Western sports that have enjoyed great recent popularity in Saudi Arabia. Snorkeling and scuba diving in the Red Sea are considered among the best in the world by sports enthusiasts. Boating and fishing are popular on both the Red Sea and Persian Gulf coasts.

Food

Although they are prohibited from eating certain foods and drinking alcohol, Saudi Arabians partake in strong and savory food and drink. Grilled chicken and roast lamb are among the dishes

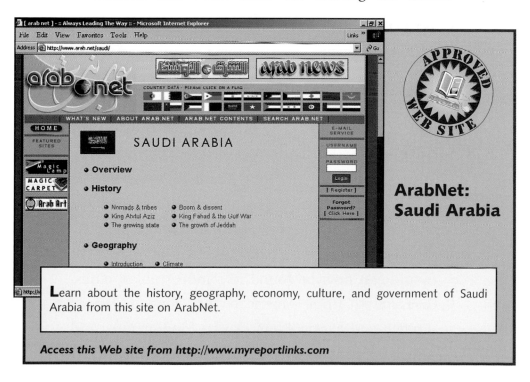

ArabNet: Saudi Arabia

Learn about the history, geography, economy, culture, and government of Saudi Arabia from this site on ArabNet.

Access this Web site from http://www.myreportlinks.com

widely enjoyed by Saudis. Especially popular is Kebsa, a dish of stewed lamb served on boiled rice. Falafel, which is deep-fried chunks of spiced and seasoned chickpeas, and fuul, a paste made from fava beans, garlic, and lemon, are also dietary staples. Camel meat is a local specialty and Arabian unleavened bread, also know as khobz, is served on the side with most meals in Saudi Arabia.

▷ Popular Drinks

Coffee beans are believed to have originated in Ethiopia, but were made famous through Arab trade networks. Arabica coffee beans are considered among the best in the world. An especially strongly brewed kind of coffee called *qahwa* is prepared and served in a highly ritualized way, based on ancient tribal customs. Strong and somewhat bitter, qahwa is not sweetened or mixed with milk, but served with dates on the side. While qahwa is an elaborately prepared, formally served beverage, Saudis prefer tea for more casual drinking. Sitting and drinking tea with a friend or family member and engaging in prolonged discussion is a favorite pastime for many Saudi people.

Restaurants with cuisine from all over the world can now be found in Saudi Arabian cities. Everything from American fast food to fancy French and exotic Asian can be found there, and the Saudi people have shown they enjoy the variety even as they maintain their own culinary culture and tradition.

Customs

Occasionally, Saudi men and women dress in colorful and elaborate garments, although it is always modest. For special occasions, men will wear a gold-embroidered cloak called a *bisht*. Men may also wear a black cord called an *igal* on their head to tie their gutra in place. Women often dress in colorful, Western-style clothing under their abayas, and at private family gatherings and

Saudi culture is very different from that in the United States. These differences can be seen in the way Saudis greet each other, their laid-back approach to life, the use of only their right hand when eating, and other daily activities. Learn more about Saudi etiquette at the **King Faisal Specialist Hospital and Research Centre: Assalaamu alaikum** Web site.

celebrations, women also sometimes wear stylish, long-flowing dresses and frilly hairpieces.

Some Saudi women have also begun wearing Western-style bridal gowns for their weddings, but in many ways, Saudi marriage has remained unchanged for centuries. Marriages are still usually arranged between senior family members. An Islamic cleric called an Imam officiates at the wedding ceremony. At wedding receptions, men and women are segregated, and other than the groom and the bride's family, no male guests can see the bride, as she is unveiled for the wedding celebration.

Muslim men may have up to four wives at a time, but they must pay a dowry—an amount of money or valuable gifts—to a woman before taking her as a wife. Divorce is permitted in Saudi Arabia. Men need simply express their desire for a divorce three times in the presence of two adult male Muslim witnesses. Under Saudi law they are entitled to custody of any children the couple have had. Women can also obtain divorces and are entitled to a portion of the family's wealth and property, but a woman must request and receive a divorce order from an Islamic cleric.

▶ A Woman's Perspective

Indeed, marriage and family life mirror most of Saudi society, as women are more limited in their options and restricted in their actions than men.

Carmen bin Ladin was raised in Western Europe but married a prominent Saudi Arabian business-man. Having lived several years in Saudi Arabia, bin Ladin became disturbed at the inequality in Saudi marriages that she witnessed. She wrote about her experiences in her book, *Inside the Kingdom: My Life in Saudi Arabia*. She described the severity under which married women live in that country:

> A wife in Saudi Arabia cannot do anything without her husband's permission. She cannot go out, cannot study, often cannot even eat at his table.

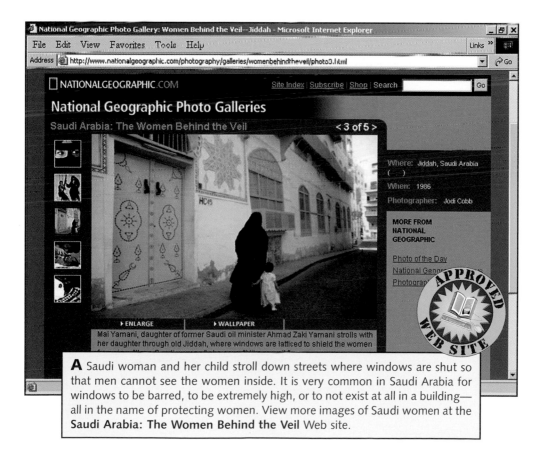

A Saudi woman and her child stroll down streets where windows are shut so that men cannot see the women inside. It is very common in Saudi Arabia for windows to be barred, to be extremely high, or to not exist at all in a building—all in the name of protecting women. View more images of Saudi women at the **Saudi Arabia: The Women Behind the Veil** Web site.

Women in Saudi Arabia must live in obedience, in isolation, and in the fear that they may be cast out and summarily divorced."[1]

The treatment of women in Saudi Arabia may seem harsh to Westerners, but there have been few expressions of discontent among Saudi women about their circumstances. The threat of severe shaming by religious authorities and legal punishment for failing to live up to expectations likely prevents many women from speaking out. There are also financial rewards for women who maintain traditional standards of behavior. As long as a woman acts honorably, her husband or his family is legally and socially obligated to support her.

There is also an attitude among both Saudi men and women that prevents them from protesting about the conditions of their lives or trying to change them. A common expression in Saudi Arabia is "Inshallah," which roughly translates to "whatever is God's will." Saudi people are likely to respond with this saying to any setback or adversity in their lives, including restrictions like those placed on women in families and marriages.

Early History

The modern Kingdom of Saudi Arabia has only existed since 1932, yet there have been people and civilizations living on the Arab Peninsula for tens of thousands of years. Arabian culture and society evolved mostly in the central desert areas of Saudi Arabia and the regions just to the north during the second millennium B.C. The nomadic customs and lifestyles that developed among the people of this area came to define and identify Arabs as a distinctive people. However, Arabs were divided by clan and tribe for hundreds of years, and often warred with each other. It was not until the emergence of Muhammad and the rise of Islam that Arabs experienced any social or political unity. When they did, they quickly rose to become a major force in the world.

The Earliest Inhabitants

Historians believe the first humans lived on the Arabian Peninsula as long as twenty thousand years ago. At that time, the peninsula had much more vegetation and moisture. These early inhabitants

▲ The Bedouin are nomadic tribespeople who live on the Arabian Peninsula. Nomadic peoples have lived in Arabia for thousands of years. This image is of a Bedouin wedding party.

were hunters and gatherers. They had a large array of plant and animal life to subsist on. Early civilizations drew many petroglyphs (pictures on stones) that depicted humans and a wide variety of animals. Archaeologists believe these pictures indicate that at one time, Saudi Arabia was more temperate in climate and supported far more plant and animal life than the present desert climate.

► Land Becomes Desert

By about 12,000 B.C., much of the land had turned to desert, and those that continued to live on the peninsula needed to resort to nomadic herding to survive, or settle near oases or coastal areas where they could raise crops. Those who lived along the coasts of the Red Sea, the Persian Gulf, and the Indian Ocean (which borders the Arabian Peninsula but not Saudi Arabia itself) benefited from a gentler climate and more fertile land. They were also located very accessibly to advanced civilizations in Egypt, Mesopotamia (in modern Iraq), and Persia (now known as Iran). The combination of the superior climate and the accessibility to the major commercial and cultural centers of the time enabled the people in these areas to develop more diverse and complex societies than that which developed in the central Peninsula. Yet it was the central Arab nomadic people, also known as the Bedouin, whose culture and society would

http://lava.nationalgeographic.com/pod/pictures/sm_wallpaper/06081_56.jpg - Microsoft Internet Explorer

File   Edit   View   Favorites   Tools   Help

Links »

Address http://lava.nationalgeographic.com/pod/pictures/sm_wallpaper/06081_56.jpg   Go

Done

Saudi Arabia was one of the first lands inhabited by the Bedouin, a nomadic Arab group. The Bedouin in Saudi Arabia are largely Sunni Muslim, and this Bedouin woman shown here wears the traditional mask, known as a burka. View more pictures of the Bedouin at the **Peoples: Bedouin** Web site.

provide the roots from which modern Saudi Arabia would grow and develop.

People in the central peninsula are referred to as Arabs in historic writings dating as far back as the ninth century B.C. Although the term generally referred to nomadic people from the area, in fact there were permanent and semipermanent settlements in central Arabia for about as long as there have been nomads. Tribal hierarchies provided strong local leadership for the people, and writing and number systems developed as early as the second millennium B.C. Yet the people in the central peninsula were neither as prosperous nor as connected to the rest of the world as those in the coastal areas. That changed sometime around the year 1000 B.C. with the adoption of the camel as a transport and cargo-carrying animal.

▶ Central Arabia Emerges

The camel has a unique ability to survive and exert itself in the desert. Sometimes it can go for weeks without consuming water. This enabled people to travel through the vast central deserts and rugged mountains that made up central Arabia. When camels started being used for transport across Arabia's central peninsula, the area's traffic, commercial activity, and prosperity greatly increased. Central Arabians came into more frequent contact with people from Europe, Asia, and Africa, as well as the people along the coasts of Arabia itself. The Bedouin became major players in what was then the known civilized world.

These people established many of the basic tenets of modern Saudi Arabian life. Governing power structures were formed around families, or clans, and networks or alliances of families that constituted tribes. Tribal leaders were called sheiks, just as they are today. Warfare and robbery between tribes and clans were common, but valor and hospitality were also important. Arabic poetry, music, and dance formed and evolved during this time. Herding and hunting of animals began on a large scale. Bedouin customs and practices spread through a wide area, both within the peninsula and beyond its natural borders.

The Islamic Empire

When inspired by the words of Muhammad and convinced that they were acting on behalf of God, the greatly divided Arabs were able to come together and build a vast empire. After Muhammad's death, Islam spread rapidly through

This wall drawing, dating back to the second or third century A.D., was found in a building located in Al Fao, an ancient village. View this and other artifacts on the Web site of **The National Museum,** located in Saudi Arabia.

EDITOR'S CHOICE

the Middle East and North Africa. A series of successors to Muhammad, who came to be known as caliphs, successfully carried Islam well across Asia and Africa within a few decades. Even parts of Europe would be conquered by Muslim armies at the height of power for the Islamic Empire. However, these successful conquests of areas distant from the original Arab homelands led to a shifting of power within the Islamic Empire away from Saudi Arabia to new power centers to the north. This shift ushered in a time when the territories on the Arabian Peninsula would come under the command of rulers and empires based in foreign lands.

Power Shifts Away From Saudi Arabia

The fourth successor to Muhammad, Ali ibn Abi Talib, took power as caliph in 656. Ali, a cousin and son-in-law of Muhammad, established his capital in a town in what is now southern Iraq called Kufa. Five years later, another caliph, Muawiya, would establish headquarters even farther to the north, in the Syrian city of Damascus. A family line of ruling power was established there. Local leaders in Saudi Arabia still had considerable power within their own regions and communities. Moreover, the leaders in the holy cities of Mecca and Medina wielded considerable power within the Islamic Empire as

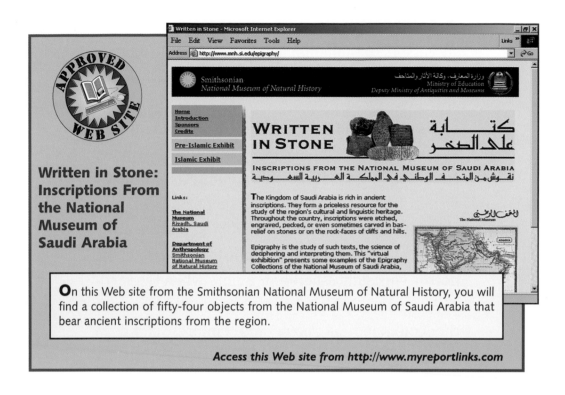

Written in Stone: Inscriptions From the National Museum of Saudi Arabia

On this Web site from the Smithsonian National Museum of Natural History, you will find a collection of fifty-four objects from the National Museum of Saudi Arabia that bear ancient inscriptions from the region.

Access this Web site from http://www.myreportlinks.com

caretakers of the sacred sites. Nevertheless, with the establishment of the ruling power of Muawiya's lineage, known as the Umayyad Dynasty, local leaders in Saudi Arabia started being subject to the rule of distant leaders. These conditions would persist in Saudi Arabia for many hundreds of years.

The Umayyad Dynasty would only last from A.D. 661 until 750. It would be replaced by another family known as the Abbasids, who also established royal lineage rights. The Abbasid Dynasty, which would move the Islamic capital to Baghdad, would last for over five hundred years. During that time, a period known as the Golden Age of

Islam occurred. This period saw great advances in scientific fields such as chemistry, medicine, and astronomy, as well as academic areas like mathematics, literature, and geography within the Islamic Empire. James Wynbrandt describes the intellectual and artistic accomplishments of the Islamic Empire in *A Brief History of Saudi Arabia:*

> The range and brilliance of its intellectual accomplishments are as astonishing as was the rapid military conquest that enabled its appearance. This was the Golden Age of Islam. It predated Europe's Renaissance (which Islamic learning would play a major role in making possible) by five hundred years. At its pinnacle . . . the empire and culture reached a level of sophistication that would be unequaled for almost 1,000 years.[1]

▶ Decline

However, with the political power base of Islam having shifted away from Saudi Arabia, so too did most of the intellectual and creative activity of the time. The holy cities of Mecca and Medina remained important to the rulers, and they took measures to ensure safe passage for pilgrims and protect the cities from hostile attack. The Hejaz area continued to benefit from trade activity due to its location along the Red Sea and its geographic closeness to Europe, Africa, and Asia. The religious cities also played an important role in the development of Sharia, the application of Islamic

▲ *These Muslims are worshipping in Mecca sometime between 1885 and 1889. Regardless of who ruled what is now Saudi Arabia, the cities of Mecca and Medina remained important holy places.*

principles to civil and state governance as well as to religious worship. For the most part, though, the great achievements and advances of the Golden Age of Islam did not originate from Saudi Arabia. The central Najd region, always difficult to access and less settled and advanced than the western Hejaz, experienced serious decline during this time. New and improved ships and sailing techniques, as well as the emergence of overland trade routes to the north, reduced the importance and affluence of Najd.

The Mamluk Era

In 1258, the Abbasid Dynasty fell to the Mongols, fierce invaders from what is now Mongolia. They were led by the historically famous Genghis and Kublai Khan. At that time, another empire based in Egypt, headed by former Turkish slaves called the Mamluks, had begun to grow. The Mamluks had taken over Egypt around 1250. They had been driven out of Arabia by the Seljuks. The Seljuks maintained control of the caliphate until the Mongol conquest. The Mamluks also came under attack by the Mongols, but they were able to prepare for the Mongol onslaught and turn back the attack. In so doing, the Mamluks gained control of Arabia. Yet little changed for the people of the peninsula, as they had become accustomed to being part of an empire that was ruled from a distant place. The Mamluks, like their predecessors in Damascus and Baghdad, paid little attention to the Arabian Peninsula. This was not to be the case with the next set of rulers over Arabia.

The Ottoman Era

The Ottomans were Muslim Turks who had taken over the historic and strategic city of Constantinople (later renamed Istanbul) in 1453. From there they expanded their power and built an empire that would last over four hundred years. After defeating the Mamluks in 1517, the Ottomans took possession of Arabia and made efforts to exert more direct control over the area. This included directly appointing the leaders of the city of Mecca, known as sharifs, who had sometimes acted independently or defiantly under previous regimes. The title "sharif" refers to someone who can claim to be a direct descendant of Muhammad.

The Ottomans also invaded and occupied the eastern part of the peninsula in the sixteenth and seventeenth centuries after having captured Baghdad. They installed other local leaders and stationed military forces along the west coast of Arabia but never penetrated the country's deeper interior sections. It was in this part of Arabia during the reign of the Ottomans that the political and religious factions and movements would

This is what remains of an Ottoman fort built in the 1800s in Saudi Arabia. Ottoman forces were driven out of Saudi Arabia in 1916.

begin that would ultimately lead to the creation of the nation of Saudi Arabia.

Foreign Domination and Disarray

Centuries of marginalization created hardship and strain in central Arabia. Tribes, clans, and villages raided and attacked each other with great frequency. According to James Wynbrandt, "Najd towns were said to be in a state of permanent warfare with one another, a characterization that extended to the other interior provinces."[2] There were also conflicts between tribes and clans of the Najd and forces from the Hejaz, especially armies under the command of the sharifs of Mecca. From the sixteenth to the eighteenth century, these armies would periodically raid, plunder, and conquer various towns and regions in the interior.

The western region of Saudi Arabia had also been under foreign domination for centuries, but it had had some advantages over the Najd and other central regions. The local leaders of Mecca had always maintained some levels of power and independence. The sacred sites of Islam received special attention and protection, and the sea and land trade routes through the region continued to be used with much more frequency than those through central Arabia. However, tribal and regional conflict also adversely affected the

Hejaz, and the imposition made by the Ottoman rulers in the region reduced or eliminated whatever independence the people there had previously known. Overall, conditions throughout Saudi Arabia were poor and unpromising in the late seventeenth and early eighteenth centuries. It was at this time that two people vital to the formation of Saudi Arabia first emerged in their historic roles.

The Roots of Modern Saudi Arabia

Saud ibn Muhammad ibn Miqrin was born about 1665 into the ruling family of the town of Diriya, which had become one of central Arabia's largest and most powerful towns. After years of instability and bloody power struggles in Diriya, Saud established stability in the town's leadership that enabled his descendants to maintain firm and steady control over it for many years after his death in 1725. Saud's son, Muhammad ibn Saud, took over Diriya in 1726 and held it until his death nearly forty years later.

It was Muhammad ibn Saud who would form the critical partnership with Muhammad ibn Abd al-Wahhab, the founder of the Wahhabi sect of Islam that is so dominant in the lives of Saudi Arabians today. Wahhab was born about 1703 into a line of Islamic clerics. He showed strong interest in religious studies at an early age, and traveled from his home in the central Arabian city of

The House of Saud refers to the rule of the Saud family, whose conquered lands were to later become known as Saudi Arabia. Learn about all aspects of Saudi life at the **Saudi Arabia Factfile** Web site.

Huraimila to the sacred cities of Mecca and Medina to study, as well as the Iraqi city of Basra. Wahhab became disturbed at what he saw as the failings of people to live up to the standards and teachings of Islam.

The outside rulers who had dominated Saudi Arabia for so long had been more focused on civil government and economic prosperity than on religion. There were many pagan practices that had been revived. Indulgence and decadence were widespread in Arabia. Wahhab preached a return to the basics of Islam and a rigidly strict interpretation of and adherence to the Qur'an and other Islamic texts.

Wahhab established himself in the large town of Uyaina, one of the major settlements of the central region. By the early 1740s, he had gained a sizable following, but when Wahhab had a woman stoned to death for confessing to adultery, many people reacted with horror. The local leader of Uyaina was pressured to exile Wahhab. It was then that Wahhab settled in Diriya, governed by Muhammad ibn Saud. Muhammad ibn Saud offered Wahhab safe haven and became a follower of his teachings. Wahhab provided Saud with religious justification for wars of conquest against other tribes, towns, and villages that did not follow strict interpretations of Islam. Saud forces from Diriya spread their power and influence and forcibly converted people to Wahhabism over the next thirty years, bringing Diriya to a position of supremacy in central Arabia.

Saud's Forces Take More Control

In 1773, Saud's forces captured the city of Riyadh. From there, Saud expanded his control over Arab territory to include much of the eastern part of the country. He also expanded his holdings to the north, toward the borders with Iraq and Jordan. Ultimately, the Wahhabi-Saud forces would conquer and occupy Mecca, but that would not sit well with the Ottoman rulers in Turkey. Perceiving the threat from Saud, the Ottoman sultans, as the leaders were known, turned their forces against those from Diriya. The Ottomans would finally defeat the Saud forces, ending the first Saudi Arabian state, when they seized and destroyed Diriya in 1818. However, the desire for unity and independence among Arabians would grow in the following years.

Modern History

The defeat of the first Saudi state by the Ottomans did not eliminate support for either the Al Saud clan or the Wahhabi form of Islam. Over the next hundred years, Saudi and Wahhabi power and influence would rise and fall before finally gaining supremacy in Saudi Arabia in 1932.

As soon as Saudi Arabia became an independent country, it was almost immediately propelled into the modern technological world by the discovery of huge crude oil reserves within its territory. The presence of this highly valuable resource in such large quantities has rapidly and dramatically transformed Saudi Arabia from primitiveness to modernism. Yet Saudi Arabians have steadfastly maintained their historic traditions, beliefs, and practices, even as their country has developed into a major world economic power and their society has become technologically progressive.

▶ Saudi and Wahhabi Resurgence

Support for the Al Saud clan and the Wahhabists was strong enough that, even after being defeated by the Ottomans, they were able to reestablish control over Riyadh in the 1820s. From there they took control of enough territory in Saudi Arabia so that historians refer to this time in the nineteenth century as the second Saudi Arabian state. However, this was neither as large nor as stable as the previous Saudi state had been. The Al Saud clan never took control of Hejaz as they had in the eighteenth century. Even within central Arabia they faced stiff challenges. Another clan, the Al Rashid, who were based in the town of Hail in the Shammar Mountains to the northwest of Riyadh, controlled considerable territory in Arabia during the second Saudi state. Smaller clans and tribes also maintained their independence. The Al Saud

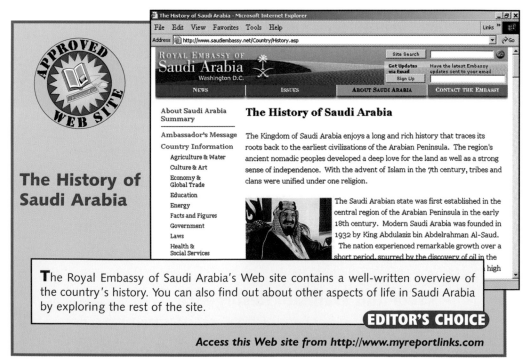

The History of Saudi Arabia

The Royal Embassy of Saudi Arabia's Web site contains a well-written overview of the country's history. You can also find out about other aspects of life in Saudi Arabia by exploring the rest of the site.

EDITOR'S CHOICE

Access this Web site from http://www.myreportlinks.com

family was also hindered by internal conflict among its own members. With all these factors working against it, the second Saudi state was fully terminated by its Rashidi rivals in the Battle of al-Mulayda in 1891. But Arabia had not heard the last of the Al Saud clan or Wahhabi Islam.

Exile

After the Saudi defeat by the Rashidis, the last Saudi ruler of Riyadh went into exile in nearby Kuwait. His son, Abd al-Aziz ibn Abd al-Rahman ibn Faisal Al Saud, commonly known simply as Ibn Saud, accompanied him. He had been born in Saudi Arabia in 1880, but spent his formative years in exile. He learned the teachings of Wahhabism at a young age and also spent time with Bedouin tribespeople, learning about warfare and desert survival techniques. Even after their banishment, the Al Sauds hoped to reestablish their power on the Arabian Peninsula, and Ibn Saud would come to share this ambition. In 1900, he began to launch forays into Saudi Arabia, and found that there was still strong support for the Al Saud clan and Wahhabism. In 1902, he recaptured Riyadh with a fighting force of just a few dozen, even though the Rashidis, who had control of Riyadh, greatly outnumbered his men. Within a few years, he had considerably extended his territory, creating the third Saudi Arabian state,

▲ As the Al Saud clan fought the Ottomans for control of their holy land, pilgrims still flocked to Mecca for the hajj. This is an image of camels and tents of the pilgrims in 1910.

the one that would ultimately become modern Saudi Arabia.

▶ Arab Rebellion and World War I

While there were many things that divided Arabians, toward the end of the nineteenth century, one thing united many of them: dislike of the Ottomans who held power over their country. Hostile feelings toward the Ottomans grew even stronger after a revolution in Turkey in 1908 brought a new group called the Young Turks to power. These new rulers showed no interest in upholding Muslim beliefs or traditions. Instead, they were focused on promoting Turkish nationalism and asserting power over their territories. Under the Young Turks, Arabs were oppressed more severely than they had been under any previous rulers. In response, strong Arab nationalism became deeply felt among the diverse people of the peninsula and among Arabs in other areas such as Syria and Iraq.

▶ Opposing the Turks

Strong opposition to Turkish domination even brought together the people of the Najd and Hejaz regions. When World War I broke out in 1914, the Ottomans, close allies of Germany, entered the war on their side, against Great Britain and France. The British took the opportunity to act against the Ottomans by encouraging Arab anger and opposition toward them. The British offered to recognize and support an independent Arab nation if the Arabs sided with them in the war. Hussein ibn Ali Al Hashimi, the sharif of Mecca at the time, responded by revolting against Ottoman troops on Arab territory. Ottoman forces were driven out of Hejaz in 1916. The British also provided financial and logistic support. T. E. Lawrence, who became famous as Lawrence of Arabia, played an important role in convincing the British government to commit themselves to assisting

Lawrence of Arabia . T.E. Lawrence | PBS - Microsoft Internet Explorer

File   Edit   View   Favorites   Tools   Help   Links »

Address http://www.pbs.org/lawrenceofarabia/players/lawrence.html   Go

PBS HOME   PROGRAMS A-Z   TV SCHEDULES   SUPPORT PBS   SHOP PBS   SEARCH PBS

Lawrence of Arabia

T.E. Lawrence

The Players

T. E. Lawrence
Prince Feisal
General Allenby
King Hussein
Dahoum
Churchill

He called himself an 'ordinary man' but Thomas Edward Lawrence lived an extraordinary life.

Born in Tremadoc, Wales, in 1888, Thomas Edward - known as Ned - was the second of five illegitimate boys.

Lawrence's father, Sir Thomas Chapman, left his first marriage when he fell in love with the family governess, Sarah Junner. His parents assumed the name of Lawrence and remained unmarried.

T. E. Lawrence will always be known as Lawrence of Arabia for his love of the Middle East and the role he played in leading the Arab army to victory over the Ottoman Empire in the early 1900s. Learn more about T. E. Lawrence and his legacy at the **Lawrence of Arabia** Web site.

the Arabs. He also advised the Arab forces in their campaign to drive the Ottomans out of Hejaz. The British likewise urged Ibn Saud in the Najd to fight against the Ottomans and their allied forces in the Arabian interior. In so doing, Ibn Saud succeeded in expanding the territory under Saudi control once again. The Ottomans were ultimately defeated, their empire of hundreds of years toppled, and the Arabian Peninsula freed from the grip of its power. The rival Najd and Hejaz Arabians had found common purpose during the war, but their long-standing and deeply rooted rivalry would resurface upon its conclusion.

▶ The Founding of Saudi Arabia

Following the war, the British mostly disregarded promises they had made concerning Arabian independence. However, people in the Arabian Peninsula were largely left to determine their own fates. The rulers of both Hejaz and Najd sought to dominate the region. While the forces of the Hejaz had shown themselves to be more effective in fighting against the Ottomans, they did not fare so well against Ibn Saud's forces. Ibn Saud had assembled an army called the *Ikhwan* (which means brethren) that was dedicated to spreading Wahhabi teaching and enforcing Wahhabi rules and standards. The Ikhwan played an important role in defeating the forces of Hejaz, giving Ibn Saud control over the region in 1925. A few territories in the distant south of Saudi Arabia had still not been conquered by Saud, but he would achieve this by 1932. He then declared the foundation of the new kingdom of Saudi Arabia, which united the Hejaz and Najd, and included other territories held by Saud as well.

▶ Oil

In 1938, oil prospectors representing American oil companies found huge reserves of crude oil. The

planet's largest known reserves were discovered
on Saudi Arabian territory. Saudi Arabia was
rapidly transformed into a modern, prosperous
nation. Commercial oil production in Saudi Arabia
began in 1939. Even with the interruption of international trade caused by World War II (1939–45),
oil production in Saudi Arabia grew tremendously
by 1945, going from five hundred thousand barrels a day to 21 million in six years. The discovery
of large amounts of oil in Saudi Arabia led to great
interest in the country by industrialized Western
nations.

United States-Saudi Relations

The United States became a major trading partner
and ally of Saudi Arabia. An American oil company, Standard Oil of California, contracted with
the Saudi government to drill for oil and refine
it. Ibn Saud met with U.S. President Franklin
Roosevelt in 1945 and agreed to join World War II
on the side of the United States. This was largely
symbolic as the war was nearly won by the Allies
at that point and Saudi Arabia had very little
to contribute in the way of armed forces. Yet, the
decision signaled the course Saudi Arabia and
the United States would take for the rest of the
twentieth century. Trade and diplomatic ties
between the two countries have been close and
extensive ever since.

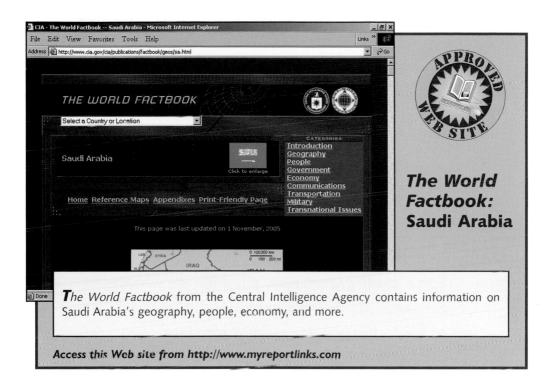

The World Factbook from the Central Intelligence Agency contains information on Saudi Arabia's geography, people, economy, and more.

Access this Web site from http://www.myreportlinks.com

▶ Saudi Government

The relationship between the United States and Saudi Arabia has been friendly in spite of dramatic differences between the nations' governments. Saudi Arabia's government is markedly different from the democracy practiced and supported by the United States. During the nation's early years, there was virtually no government in Saudi Arabia except the ruling Saudi family. Over time, other branches of Saudi government have developed, although absolute power remains with the king to override decisions and actions of any other branch of government. A Council of Ministers is appointed by the king. It advises him and makes some administrative and legislative decisions. This consists of about forty members. Another body called the Consultative Council advises the Council of Ministers. This council is larger and meant to be more representative of the general population.

There are thirteen provinces in Saudi Arabia that each have an appointed governor and deputy governor. Beneath these officials are provincial councils appointed by the governors. Only at the local level are there any elections in Saudi Arabia. Some local government advisors are chosen in elections, but only about half of the total number of such officials. Even these elections were suspended from the 1970s until 2005. Hopes were raised that the renewed elections might allow women to participate for the first time, but it turned out women were not permitted to vote. Even participation among men was disappointingly low.

▶ The Courts

All government decisions are subject to approval by senior Muslim clerics known as the Ulama. Because Saudi Arabia is governed based on the Qur'an and Islamic law, the word of the Ulama is critical. Saudi courts are also based on the Sharia, the body of Islamic law derived from the Qur'an and the Hadith. Saudi courts consist of first instance and appeals courts. Civil and criminal cases are first tried in courts of first instance. Their

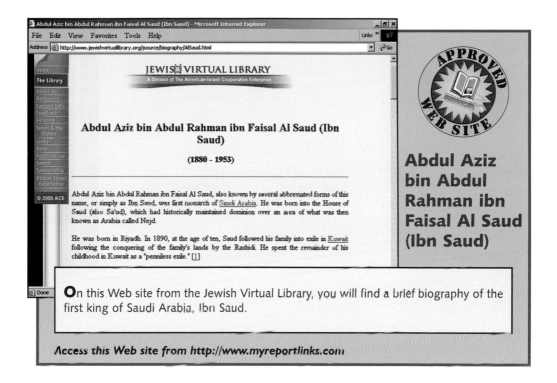

Abdul Aziz bin Abdul Rahman ibn Faisal Al Saud (Ibn Saud) - Microsoft Internet Explorer

File   Edit   View   Favorites   Tools   Help   Links »

Address http://www.jewishvirtuallibrary.org/jsource/biography/AlSaud.html   Go

JEWISH VIRTUAL LIBRARY
A Division of The American-Israeli Cooperative Enterprise

Abdul Aziz bin Abdul Rahman ibn Faisal Al Saud (Ibn Saud)

(1880 - 1953)

Abdul Aziz bin Abdul Rahman ibn Faisal Al Saud, also known by several abbreviated forms of this name, or simply as Ibn Saud, was first monarch of Saudi Arabia. He was born into the House of Saud (also Sa'ud), which had historically maintained dominion over an area of what was then known as Arabia called Nejd.

He was born in Riyadh. In 1890, at the age of ten, Saud followed his family into exile in Kuwait following the conquering of the family's lands by the Rashidi. He spent the remainder of his childhood in Kuwait as a "penniless exile." [1]

Abdul Aziz bin Abdul Rahman ibn Faisal Al Saud (Ibn Saud)

On this Web site from the Jewish Virtual Library, you will find a brief biography of the first king of Saudi Arabia, Ibn Saud.

Access this Web site from http://www.myreportlinks.com

decisions can then be appealed to and reviewed by the appeals courts. The king can also appoint special courts and tribunals to handle issues not addressed by the Sharia.

▶ Becoming a Major World Nation

Saudi Arabia's importance as the land of the founding of Islam has continued during modern times. The great importance of crude oil as a resource has also bolstered Saudi Arabia's position in the world. Although Saudi Arabia has mostly allied itself with Western powers, particularly the United States, relations between the two countries have not been trouble free. Even while Ibn Saud

▲ *American and European workers began to control Saudi Arabia's oil industry in the 1930s. Bechtel is one of the corporations that was prominent in the region. This is an image of a small city built by the Bechtel Corporation in Saudi Arabia.*

was still in power, the two countries had sharp differences. The creation of the nation of Israel in the Middle East and the United States's support for Israel in wars it fought against its Arab neighbors in the late 1940s were major causes of this disagreement. Saudi Arabia did not participate in the military combat but did provide assistance to the Arab countries fighting Israel in those wars.

Ibn Saud died in 1953 and was succeeded by his son Saud bin Abdul Aziz. He quickly stirred disapproval both from within Saudi Arabia and internationally by spending money on himself and the royal family. The common people thought he was neglecting the growth and development of the country. Dislike of American control of the oil industry also arose during the 1950s. Many local people hired by the oil companies felt they were overworked and underpaid. Throughout the country, people were unhappy that wealth derived from their nation was helping the royal family and the king's foreign allies but not the common Saudi people. Opponents organized and held demonstrations, but the Saudi government responded with arrests and violence. Financial mismanagement and domestic disturbances brought pressure on Saud to abdicate to his half brother Faisal bin Abdul Aziz in 1958. However, Saud immediately began attempting to recapture power. Saud and Faisal jousted for leadership of the country over the next few years, the crown alternating between them until Faisal took power for good in 1964.

Faisal's Reign

During his time in power, Faisal made efforts to improve living conditions and the infrastructure in Saudi Arabia. Excess spending on royal luxury was cut, and more was devoted to education, health care, roads, and communications networks. The money from the sale of oil paid for these works. Saudi Arabia's wealth especially expanded in the early 1970s. This was due to a surge in oil prices caused by an embargo by Arab oil-producing nations against major Western nations that had been supportive of Israel. This was a low point in Saudi-American relations, as the Saudi government supported the embargo and cut its oil production. This caused a surge upward in oil prices that brought in vast new wealth to Saudi Arabia. Education and health care were made available throughout the country. Airports and urban centers were enlarged and modernized. The capital city of Riyadh and the airports at Riyadh and Jeddah have become among the

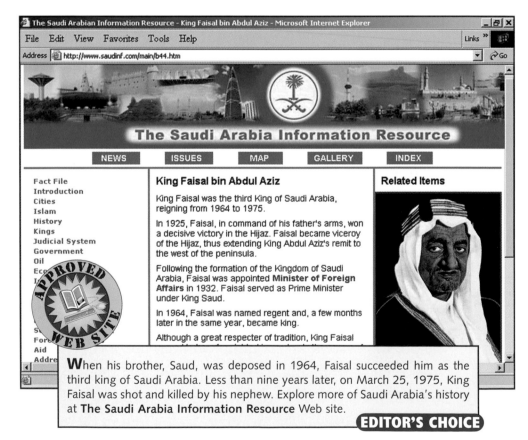

The Saudi Arabian Information Resource - King Faisal bin Abdul Aziz - Microsoft Internet Explorer

File   Edit   View   Favorites   Tools   Help   Links

Address http://www.saudinf.com/main/b44.htm   Go

The Saudi Arabia Information Resource

NEWS   ISSUES   MAP   GALLERY   INDEX

Fact File
Introduction
Cities
Islam
History
Kings
Judicial System
Government
Oil
Ec
I

S
For
Aid
Addre

King Faisal bin Abdul Aziz

King Faisal was the third King of Saudi Arabia, reigning from 1964 to 1975.

In 1925, Faisal, in command of his father's arms, won a decisive victory in the Hijaz. Faisal became viceroy of the Hijaz, thus extending King Abdul Aziz's remit to the west of the peninsula.

Following the formation of the Kingdom of Saudi Arabia, Faisal was appointed **Minister of Foreign Affairs** in 1932. Faisal served as Prime Minister under King Saud.

In 1964, Faisal was named regent and, a few months later in the same year, became king.

Although a great respecter of tradition, King Faisal

Related Items

When his brother, Saud, was deposed in 1964, Faisal succeeded him as the third king of Saudi Arabia. Less than nine years later, on March 25, 1975, King Faisal was shot and killed by his nephew. Explore more of Saudi Arabia's history at **The Saudi Arabia Information Resource** Web site.

EDITOR'S CHOICE

most technologically advanced in the world since that time. Even whole new industrial cities were built, notably Jubail on the Persian Gulf coast and Yanbu on the Red Sea.

Relations With the West

Lured by the promise of greater military support and supplies, Faisal reconciled with the United States in the mid-1970s. He increased oil production to help bring gas and oil prices down. Faisal was assassinated in 1975 and succeeded by Khalid ibn Abd al-Aziz, who served until 1982. He was replaced by Fahd ibn Abd al-Aziz, who continued to serve into the twenty-first century, although many of the king's duties were transferred to Crown Prince Abdullah bin Abd al-Aziz in 1995 when Fahd suffered a stroke.

Under both Khalid and Fahd, a partnership with the United States continued based on the export of oil from Saudi Arabia and the sale of military equipment to that country from the United States. Under Fahd, Saudi Arabia emerged as a leading Arab supporter of making peace between the Arabs and Israelis, a long-standing foreign policy goal of the United States. Along with several other nations, the United States and Saudi Arabia also worked together in both the Iran-Iraq War of the 1980s and the first Persian Gulf War against Iraq in the early 1990s. In both conflicts, the

American-Saudi alliance resulted in an outcome favorable for both countries. The stationing of United States forces on Saudi soil in 1990, however, led to new strains in the relationship. Hence doubt has been cast upon the future course of Saudi relations with the United States and the rest of the world.

▶ Renewed Tension

Difficulties in relations between Saudi Arabia and the West stemmed from a number of events occurring in the 1990s and 2000s. Terrorists launched recurring attacks against Saudi Arabia, the United States, Europe, and other nations that declared themselves against terrorist groups such as al-Qaeda. The terrorists were upset that the Saudi Arabian government continued to allow United States troops to be stationed on Saudi soil. Saudi Arabia did not join the war effort against Iraq led by the United States in 2003, and Saudi Arabia came under increased pressure and scrutiny from leaders of Western nations as ties between prominent Saudis and violent terrorist groups came to light. Among those expressing doubt and disapproval of Saudi Arabia were members of the U.S. Congress and the United States president. United States Senator Charles Schumer of New York wrote a letter to the Saudi ambassador to the United States in 2003, complaining about the Saudi interior minister, Prince Nayef. Schumer accused Nayef of "suborning terrorist financing and ignoring the evidence when it comes to investigating terrorist attacks on Americans."[1]

In his 2005 State of the Union Address, President George W. Bush implied that he wanted to see greater democratic reform in that country by saying "Saudi Arabia can demonstrate its leadership in the [Middle East] by expanding the role of its people in determining their future."[2]

Some Saudi Arabian people, including those working for reform and to deter terrorism within

▲ An image of future Saudi Arabian kings Faisal and Khalid. At the time this photo was taken in about 1941, they were both Amirs (Princes), while their father, King Saud, was on the throne.

**BBC News:
Middle East**

This Web site from the BBC provides all the latest news from the Middle East, including Saudi Arabia.

Access this Web site from http://www.myreportlinks.com

the country, objected to comments like these from American officials. They felt that Saudi citizens would see them as outside interference and that conservative, anti-American factions in Saudi Arabia would be strengthened by this reaction.

Officially, the trade and diplomatic relations that the United States and other Western nations have had with Saudi Arabia have remained the same as they have been for decades. But the potential for troubled future relations looms large as terrorist attacks involving Saudi extremists and efforts to aggressively combat Islamic terrorism both continue with no signs of letting up.

Business, Agriculture, and Future Outlook

the future of

As long as the world depends heavily upon crude oil for energy, Saudi Arabia will remain a world nation of major importance. The nation is also trying to diversify its economy, making use of other natural resources and adapting to modern technologies. Many people work in government service jobs, and the ruling family has spent heavily from oil revenues to provide employment and benefits to the nation's people. Yet inequality in economic conditions is a cause of increasing discontent in Saudi Arabia. Aside from concern over Saudi involvement in terrorism, criticism over the Saudi government's treatment of its people is also rising.

▶ **Industry** *there are many products such as . . . . that we get from Saudi*

Crude oil drilling and production is far and away the most important part of Saudi Arabia's economy. In 2004, Saudi Arabia pumped over 3 billion barrels of oil, the most of any nation. Nearly 90 percent of this oil was exported. Natural gas is also abundant in Saudi Arabia, and production

Life and Commerce in Saudi Arabia 7/30/2002 - Microsoft Internet Explorer

File   Edit   View   Favorites   Tools   Help   Links »

Address   http://www.time.com/time/photoessays/saudi/7.html   Go

TIME   HOME | NATION | WORLD | BUSINESS | ARTS | PHOTOS | CURRENT ISSUE   SEARCH TIME   GO

Home | 1 | 2 | 3 | 4 | 5 | 6 | | 8 | 9 | 10 | 11 | 12 | 13 | 14 | Next > >   photoessay

Life and Commerce in Saudi Arabia

Photographs for TIME by Christopher Morris/VII

A worker supervises at a crude oil loading facility at the Saudi Arabia National Oil Company, ARAMCO. The country today provides 8 percent of the oil consumed by America

◀ PREVIOUS

Try 4 issues of TIME

CHRISTOPHER MORRIS/VII FOR TIME

MORE PH

Attack in

This worker supervises oil operations in Saudi Arabia. The country has one fourth of world's oil reserves and is the leading producer and exporter of oil. This is not expected to change any time soon. View images of modern society in Saudi Arabia at the **Life and Commerce in Saudi Arabia** Web site.

and exportation of that resource has been growing significantly in recent years. In addition to energy resource production, the country also has large cement, steel, and fertilizer production industries. Mining is another major industry in Saudi Arabia. Gold and silver are among the valuable metals found in large quantities, along with bauxite, copper, iron, lead, and tin.

A number of geological and ecological projects represent a significant part of Saudi Arabia's industry. Deep underground water is extracted for drinking and irrigation in the vast Saudi desert.

Desalination, the process of removing salt from seawater, is also a major industry in Saudi Arabia. The largest desalination plant in the country is the Shoaiba plant located in Jeddah.

Services and Technology

The modernization programs Saudi Arabia has undertaken have also resulted in millions of Saudis employed in public service sectors. Education, health care, and community aid programs have undergone large growth since the nation started reaping great income from oil. In fact, the government is the single biggest employer in Saudi Arabia. Almost 40 percent of the population work for the government in some capacity. Electronics and telecommunications jobs have also grown substantially. There are even many women working in these fields; although, because of strict Saudi social customs, men and women do not usually share the same work spaces. Instead, women tend to specialize in servicing and dealing with other women in Saudi society. Women doctors and dentists tend to women patients; women tech support people are dedicated exclusively to assisting women computer users.

Agriculture

Modernization and technological advances have expanded Saudi Arabia's agricultural production.

This man is a Saudi Arabian teacher near Dhahran, Saudi Arabia. The traditional headscarf helps protect him from the sun.

Once limited to the few oasis areas and fertile sections along the Red Sea, crop growing is now more widespread, thanks to irrigation, underground water pumping, and desalination of seawater. In the past, Saudi Arabia's only major crops were dates, which were and remain a major export product, and citrus fruits. With the expansion of arable land, other fruits such as melons, tomatoes, and grapes, as well as wheat and other grains, are also being grown in large quantities. Some of these products are exported to smaller neighboring desert countries, but Saudi Arabia still imports a considerable portion of its produce. Sheep and chickens are the leading farm animals bred and raised for meat. Dairy farming is also very important. Saudi Arabia is home to the largest single dairy farm in the world. Thoroughbred horse breeding is an ancient activity in Saudi Arabia, and Arabian racehorses are among the fastest and most famous in the world.

Pilgrimage Economy

Even before the advent of Islam in Saudi Arabia, Mecca was a destination for pilgrims. The sacred stone in the Great Mosque (also known as the Holy Mosque) was originally an object of reverence for pagans. The ritual was adapted by Muslims, and after Islam spread to distant parts of the world, the throngs of people who would come

Background
Note:
Saudi Arabia

Saudi Arabia (08/05) - Microsoft Internet Explorer

File   Edit   View   Favorites   Tools   Help   Links »

Address   http://www.state.gov/r/pa/ei/bgn/3584.htm   Go

Home | Contact Us | Email this Page | FOIA | Privacy Notice | Archive | Español   Search

U.S. DEPARTMENT of STATE

About the   Press and   Travel and   Countries   International   History, Education   Business   Other   Employ
State Dept.   Public Affairs   Living Abroad   and Regions   Issues   and Culture   Center   Services

Bureau of Public Affairs > Electronic Information and Publications Office > Backgro

Bureau of Near Eastern Affairs
August 2005

| People |
| History |
| Government |
| Political Conditions |
| Economy |
| Foreign Relations |

Background Note: Saudi Arabia

PROFILE

OFFICIAL NAME:
Kingdom of Saudi Arabia

Geography

This up-to-date Web site from the Bureau of Foreign Affairs contains information on Saudi Arabia. Politics and the economy are the two main focal points.

Access this Web site from http://www.myreportlinks.com

to Mecca every year would provide an infusion of money into the local economy. Travel support and services are still a major aspect of western Saudi Arabia's economy. The hajj brings the most visitors to Mecca, over 2 million per year at the start of the twenty-first century. Smaller numbers of pilgrims come throughout the year, on journeys called umrahs, which can be made at any time and are less formal than the highly ritualized hajj. Muslim pilgrims also frequently visit Medina, and Jeddah's seaport and airport are major points of entry for these masses of travelers. Accommodation, food and drink, and travel guidance for these people has long been a major business in and around the areas of Islam's holy sites. Local businesses are estimated to collect billions of dollars of income from pilgrimages to the holy cites.

Internal Tensions and Discontent

In spite of Saudi Arabia's vast wealth resources, there are still economic problems within the country. Among the Saudi population there is a large imbalance in wealth and standards of living that has contributed to social tensions. For many years, a large portion of the best-paying technical and professional jobs went to foreigners. This was because there were not enough well-trained and educated Saudis to handle many of the jobs. With strong expansion and improvements of education in Saudi Arabia, more Saudis have been able to obtain these jobs.

Still, a large number of foreigners, including about thirty thousand Americans, continue to live and work in Saudi Arabia. They have a standard of living that is higher than most of the locals. By residing in enclaves specializing in serving Westerners, these foreigners are even able to engage in activities such as drinking alcohol and mixing with members of the opposite sex. These are expressly forbidden by Wahhabism and are outlawed for most people in Saudi Arabia.

On the other hand, Saudi Arabia has also imported a vast number of foreign workers to handle menial and other low-paying jobs. These are jobs that Saudis are reluctant to do. Often, they arrive from such places as India, Pakistan, the Philippines, and North Africa. These workers have come to be a permanent underclass in Saudi society. Many of these foreign workers are domestic servants who some international observers claim are treated little better than slaves. Efforts to improve the education and skills of Saudi workers do not improve the status or hopes of low-paid foreign workers. Shi'a Muslims in Saudi Arabia also tend to be mostly employed in relatively low-paying labor jobs. Discontent among these groups is growing, and there have been frequent calls for

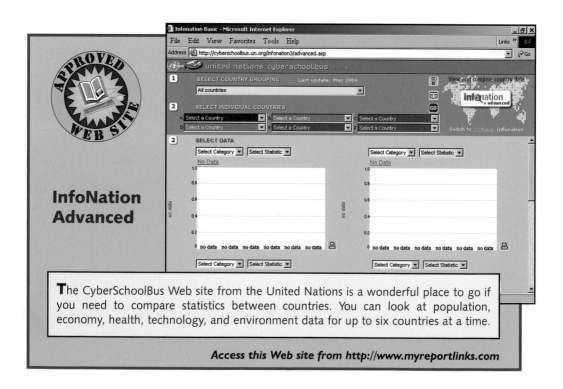

InfoNation Advanced

The CyberSchoolBus Web site from the United Nations is a wonderful place to go if you need to compare statistics between countries. You can look at population, economy, health, technology, and environment data for up to six countries at a time.

Access this Web site from http://www.myreportlinks.com

improvements in the living standards of low-level workers in recent years.

The Royal Family Under Fire

The Al Saud family has maintained stable and powerful control of its country for most of a century. They have also taken the nation through a phase of phenomenal economic growth and cultural and technological transformation. Under Al Saud governance, Saudi Arabia has risen to become a globally important nation. Yet opinion among international observers on prospects for stability in Saudi Arabia and continued Al Saud rule are divided. Journalist Martin Perctz believes the Saudi royal family cannot hold power over the long term. Writing in the magazine the *New Republic* following the 9/11 attacks, he said,

> The Saudi party, I suspect, will soon be over. Since September 11 we have begun learning how the Saudi elite funded a fanatical Wahhabi clerisy that spread its poison throughout the Muslim world. But sooner or later, the zealots will turn their attention back home, to the [Saudi rulers] they so revile.[1]

On the other hand, Middle East Studies professor F. Gregory Gause III is not so sure the Al Saud leadership will be deposed. Writing in the journal *Current History*, he points out that the regime has

▲ *Students learn in one of the schools built by Aramco, the largest oil company in Saudi Arabia. The nation continues to search for ways to adapt to the modern world while retaining its strict Muslim values.*

survived tough times before yet remained in power:

> The Saudi rulers have faced significant challenges in the past. . . . They weathered each challenge. The current threats they face could be the most serious, because they question the religious legitimacy that has underpinned the monarchy since

its founding. It would be unwise to bet against the Saudi monarchy, based on its track record of staying in power. But the odds are getting shorter.[2]

Just what course Saudi Arabia would take should the royal family fall from power would be watched intently by the entire world. Given the great value of the nation's resources, the historic instability of the Middle East region, and the willingness of terrorists from the region to resort to extreme violence, war breaking out for control of Saudi Arabia has to be considered a real, and disturbing, possibility.

Back   Forward   Stop   Review   Home   Explore   Favorites   History

Report Links

The Internet sites described below can be accessed at
http://www.myreportlinks.com

▶**The Saudi Arabia Information Resource**
Editor's Choice View this official government Web site to learn more about Saudi Arabia.

▶**Country Profile: Saudi Arabia**
Editor's Choice Examine a profile of Saudi Arabia.

▶**Perry-Castañeda Library Map Collection: Saudi Arabia Maps**
Editor's Choice View present-day and historical maps of Saudi Arabia.

▶**The History of Saudi Arabia**
Editor's Choice Read a history of Saudi Arabia from its American embassy's Web site.

▶**The National Museum**
Editor's Choice ** Take a virtual tour of the National Museum in Saudi Arabia.

▶**Ministry of Education: About Saudi Arabia**
Editor's Choice This Web site takes a look at Saudi Arabia and its people.

▶**Abdul Aziz bin Abdul Rahman ibn Faisal Al Saud (Ibn Saud)**
Learn about the first king of Saudi Arabia.

▶**Analysis: Inside Wahhabi Islam**
On this Web site you will get a better understanding of Wahhabi Islam.

▶**ArabNet: Saudi Arabia**
This Web site provides general information on Saudi Arabia.

▶**Background Note: Saudi Arabia**
Travelers to Saudi Arabia should check out this site from the U.S. State Department.

▶**BBC News: Middle East**
Read the latest news from Saudi Arabia and the Middle East.

▶**CNN: World/Middle East**
Get the latest news from the Middle East at the Cable News Network.

▶**Commanding Heights: Saudi Arabia**
Learn about the economic health of Saudi Arabia.

▶*Frontline:* **Saudi Time Bomb?**
Take a look at the affects of Islamic extremism on Saudi Arabia.

▶**InfoNation Advanced**
The United Nations provides statistics on countries from around the world.

Report Links

The Internet sites described below can be accessed at
http://www.myreportlinks.com

▶**Into the Kingdom: The Religion, Culture, & Politics of Saudi Arabia**
An inside look at life in Saudi Arabia.

▶**King Faisal Specialist Hospital and Research Centre: Assalaamu alaikum**
Find out about the most common greeting used in Saudi Arabia.

▶**Lawrence of Arabia**
Read about T. E. Lawrence and his role in the Arab revolt.

▶**Life and Commerce in Saudi Arabia**
View a photo essay from *Time* magazine.

▶**Mecca, Saudi Arabia**
Read about the city of Mecca.

▶**Muhammad Ibn Abd al-Wahab (1703–1791)**
Learn more about the founder of Wahhabi Islam.

▶**Osama bin Laden**
Read a biography of Osama bin Laden on this Web site.

▶**Peoples: Bedouin**
The Bedouin are considered to be one of the first Arab groups.

▶**Religion & Ethics: Islam**
Learn more about the Islam religion.

▶**Saudi Arabia Factfile**
This Web site takes a look at Saudi life and the popular sports in Saudi Arabia.

▶**Saudi Arabia: Places to Visit**
View some of the important holy sites located throughout Saudi Arabia.

▶**Saudi Arabia: The Women Behind the Veil**
This site from *National Geographic* gives a glimpse into the life of Saudi Arabian women.

▶**The *Saudi Gazette***
Get the latest news from this daily newspaper Web site from Saudi Arabia.

▶***The World Factbook:* Saudi Arabia**
Learn more about Saudi Arabia from this CIA Web site.

▶**Written in Stone: Inscriptions from the National Museum of Saudi Arabia**
View a collection of ancient Middle Eastern inscriptions.

al-Qaeda—An Islamist terrorist organization that claimed responsibility for the September 11, 2001 attacks, as well as other attacks on Western nations. In English, al-Qaeda translates to "the base."

Arabian Peninsula—A peninsula in the Middle East that contains the nations of Saudi Arabia, Yemen, and other Persian Gulf states.

ardha—The national dance of Saudi Arabia. In this dance, men carrying swords dance shoulder to shoulder.

Bedouin—A nomadic people who live in Arabia, Syria, and other places in the Middle East.

calligraphy—Elegant form of handwriting that traces its origins to peoples of the Arabian Peninsula.

deviant—Strange, or outside of the mainstream or what is normal.

dhubb—A type of lizard found in Saudi Arabia.

frankincense—A type of resin that is used in perfumes, embalming, or burned during religious rituals.

gutras—A headdress worn mainly in the Middle East that covers the head and shoulders but leaves an opening for the face.

hijacker—Someone who steals a plane or a vehicle from the person controlling it, usually at gunpoint or by using another type of weapon.

minarets—A tall, thin tower of a mosque that has a balcony from which prayers are shouted.

moderate—One who is not extreme and favors doing things in the mainstream.

monotheism—The belief that there is only one god.

Mutawwa—The religious police force of Saudi Arabia. They punish people who stray from the teachings of Wahabbi Islam.

myrrh—A resin with a very sharp taste.

oasis—An area with water and vegetation in an otherwise dry desert.

pagan—A follower of a religion that worships more than one god.

Qasida—Form of poetry that originated in Arabia before the days of Islam. It is also called the ode. These poems were long—usually fifty or more lines—and rarely rhymed.

rites—Religious ceremonies.

salt flat—An area were a layer of salt has formed after water dried up.

secular—Outside of religious control.

sharif—A person of nobility or importance in the Arab world, usually a descendant of Muhammad.

wadis—A streambed that only contains water during the rainy season.

Wahhabi—Member of a form of Islam that was preached by Muhammad ibn-Abdul Wahhab.

Zoroastrianism—A religion founded in Persia (modern-day Iran) by a man named Zoroaster. It was one of the first religions to preach the worship of just one god. In this case, the god was named Ahura Mazda.

Saudi Arabia Facts

1. Central Intelligence Agency, "Flag of Saudi Arabia," *The World Factbook,* November 1, 2005, <http://www.cia.gov/cia/publications/factbook/flags/sa-flag.html> (December 29, 2005).

Chapter 1. Modernism, Islamic Tradition, and Terrorism

1. James Wynbrandt, *A Brief History of Saudi Arabia* (New York: Facts on File, 2004), p. xvii.

2. Ibid., p. 256.

3. Robert Baer, *Sleeping With the Devil: How Washington Sold Our Soul for Saudi Crude* (New York: Crown Publishers, 2003), p. 21.

Chapter 2. Land, Climate, and Ecology

1. James Wynbrandt, *A Brief History of Saudi Arabia* (New York: Facts on File, 2004), p. 71.

2. Donovan Webster, "Empty Quarter: Exploring Arabia's Legendary Sea of Sand," February 2005, <http://magma.nationalgeographic.com/ngm/0502/feature1/> (December 29, 2005).

Chapter 3. Religion

1. Michael Hart, *The 100: A Ranking of the Most Influential People in History* (New York: Gallahad Books, 1982), p. 39.

2. In order to limit the numbers of pilgrims to manageable proportions, the Saudi government has introduced a quota system for pilgrim visas based on the number of inhabitants a country

has on a ration of one visa per one thousand inhabitants. With regard to inhabitants of Saudi Arabia, there is also the restriction that one may only make the Hajj every five years.

3. As another indication of the importance of Saudi control over the holy places, the previous king of Saudi Arabia, King Fahd (who ruled from 1982–2005), introduced a new title for himself: "Custodian of the Two Holy Mosques" instead of "His Majesty the King."

Chapter 4. Culture and Lifestyle

1. Carmen Bin Ladin, *Inside the Kingdom: My Life in Saudi Arabia* (New York: Time Warner, 2004), p. 67.

Chapter 5. Early History

1. James Wynbrandt, *A Brief History of Saudi Arabia* (New York: Facts on File, 2004), p. 74.

2. Ibid, p. 105.

Chapter 6. Modern History

1. Quoted in Timothy O'Brien, "Senators Push Saudi Arabia to Improve Antiterrorism Efforts," *New York Times,* August 1, 2003, p. A18.

2. George W. Bush, "State of the Union 2005," *The White House,* February 2, 2005, <http://www.whitehouse.gov/news/releases/2005/02/20050202-11.html> (December 29, 2005).

Chapter 7. Business, Agriculture, and Future Outlook

1. Martin Peretz, "Veiled Threat; Remembering Saudi Arabia," *New Republic,* January 28, 2002, p. 12.

2. F. Gregory Gause III, "Saudi Arabia Challenged," *Current History,* January 2004, vol. 103, no. 669, p. 24.

Broberg, Catherine. *Saudi Arabia in Pictures*. Minneapolis: Lerner Publications, 2003.

Cheshire, Gerard. *The Middle East*. Broomall, Pa.: Mason Crest Publishers, 2003.

Ganeri, Anita. *The Quran and Islam*. Mankato, Minn.: Smart Apple Media, 2003.

Goodwin, William. *Saudi Arabia*. San Diego, Calif.: Lucent Books, 2001.

Harper, Robert A. *Saudi Arabia*. Philadelphia: Chelsea House Publishers, 2003.

Heinrichs, Ann. *Saudi Arabia*. New York: Children's Press, 2002.

Hunt, Janin and Margaret Besher. *Saudi Arabia*. Tarrytown, N.Y.: Marshall Cavendish, 2003.

Marston, Elsa. *Muhammad of Mecca: Prophet of Islam*. New York: Franklin Watts, 2001.

Stair, Nancy L. *A Historical Atlas of Saudi Arabia*. New York: Rosen Publishing Group, 2003.

Wolf, Alex. *Osama bin Laden*. Minneapolis: Lerner Publications, 2004.